Navigating the matrix of my life has been
in *The Eternal Bond*. The book opened my
higher importance than the ministry resu

Dan Boone – Campus Director, Cru

Need help in deepening your relationship with God? New insights? Practical
advice? David English's own life and pursuit of God, captured in his book *The
Eternal Bond*, offers a wealth of wisdom to draw you closer to the God you love. I
highly recommend it.

Dr. Robert Lewis – Pastor, Founder of Men's Fraternity

I believe this book reflects David English's God-given voice in communicating
timeless, biblical truths in a powerful and compelling manner. The practical insights
in *The Eternal Bond* are guiding me into a new, deeper level of intimacy with God.
As I share these principles with other men in small groups, I observe men hungry to
apply these insights in cultivating their relationship with God.

Dick Nervig – Former Superintendent, South O'Brian School District (1A)
Spirit Lake, Iowa

We live in a world where there is constant pressure to achieve and accomplish
more and our identity is often determined by position, title or production. These
same feelings can easily permeate my relationship with God. *The Eternal Bond* is
a refreshing reminder that God loves me for who I am, and not for what I do for
Him. I am encouraged to never forsake my first love for Christ.

Jeremy Bollens – Campus Director, Cru Texas Tech University

Every Christian should read this amazing book. David English lays out Christ's
greatest commandment to love God with all of our heart, soul, and mind and to
love our neighbor as ourself. Then he tells us "how" God wants us to do that. This
message has been on David's heart as long as I've known him. David gives practical
steps on how to love (bond with) God and how to, in turn, love those whom God
places in your life. Do yourself a favor. Read this book and then live what it says.

Don Meredith – President and Founder, Christian Family Life
Author, *Two Becoming One*

The Eternal Bond was a much needed refocusing point for me as I looked at my
future and wanted to process where I desired to be in 30 years. Even in a Christian
subculture, it's easy to get caught up in results and doing. David English captures
the essence of walking with God for the sake of knowing Him. *The Eternal Bond*
speaks of intimacy with God and intimacy with Him in mission as the foundation
of God's creation of us.

Toby Vaughn – Campus Director, Cru North Dallas

When I ask, "What is God's plan for my life?," I am really wanting direction on
a specific decision – what job should I take, should I make this move, make this
investment, etc. What I am really longing for is the purpose of my life. David does
an incredible service to us all in explaining in a fresh and new way that intimacy
with God is the purpose of life. David has helped me see that experiencing
intimacy with God is of far greater value than any accomplishment I can achieve.
This perspective has set me on a new journey with Christ!

Gary Maxwell – Chief Supply Chain Officer, Dollar Tree / Family Dollar

No matter where you are in your journey with the Lord, there are insights and nuggets in David's book, *The Eternal Bond*, to encourage, guide and help you along the way. David English, like the biblical David, is a man after God's own heart. His book is profound, grace-filled, and honest.

Ney Bailey – Author, Speaker, Cru

If, like me, you have a tendency to get caught up in comparison, competition, performance, and appearance, you will delight in this exploration to a deeper intimacy and purpose. What makes *The Eternal Bond* special is that it not only lays out a compelling vision to wake us up to what life is all about, but it also articulates practical ways to cultivate and pursue this type of bonding with God and others. As you read, you will experience a desire to live a deeper and more connected story. *The Eternal Bond* excels in offering pathways with tangible implications.

David Robbins – Director of Millennials, Cru New York City

Powerful explanations, practical applications, and workable building blocks for anyone who seeks to get serious in their walk with God. David's *The Eternal Bond* book will have you exploring and wanting to grow in that special relationship that is like no other. And tell you how!

Dr. William H. Cook – Author of *Success, Motivation, and the Scriptures*

The Eternal Bond has had a profound affect on how I see and experience God! David shares, in simple terms, how we can cultivate and nurture a deep, intimate, bonded relationship with Jesus Christ.

Brandon Boyd – Cru Oklahoma State University

The Eternal Bond has truly had a huge impact on my life and has helped me evaluate my purpose and relationship with Christ. I currently use this book in my ministry as well as using it in our local church to launch all of our Men's Groups. I highly encourage you to read it and process its truths with a group of men.

Jon Foltz – National Director, Leadership Development,
Campus Crusade for Christ Thailand

For over 20 years, David English has explored how we can make intimacy with God the focus of our lives. Through this dedicated effort, he has also explored how we can make intimacy with God to be the focus of our ministry and vocation, our stewardship, and our rest. *The Eternal Bond* shares with the reader the results of that exploration into the believer's best place in the glory of God. Its insights are very useful because they are grounded in the witness of what David has learned from his own experience in this very quest.

Dr. William Kendrick, MD – Family Medicine

Intimacy with God is the end game and the key to living a full life. *The Eternal Bond* is an incredible tool that will help you to grow and deepen the relationship that matters most. David lays out a powerful process that will help you to focus on the One Thing!

Dave Runyon – Co-author of *The Art of Neighboring*

David English is not only the author of this book, but he has lived it out the past 40 years of ministry. I have personally walked a spiritual journey with him the past 10 years. He has truly helped me understand the purpose of life is intimacy with Christ, and all ministry we have is a grace gift from God.

Scott Page – Director of Development, Help One Now

DEEPLY CONECTING YOU
TO GOD AND OTHERS

THE ETERNAL BOND

DAVID A. ENGLISH

The Eternal Bond

© 2016 David A. English

Published by
Gravitation
3921 Lake Ferry Drive, Raleigh, NC 27606

Cover and book design – Larry Thompson

Printed in the United States of America

All Scripture quotations, unless otherwise indicated, are taken from the New American Standard Bible. ©1960, 1962, 1963, 1968, 1971, 1972, 1973, 1975, 1977, 1995 by the Lockman Foundation.

ISBN: 978-0-578-17641-3

THE
ETERNAL
BOND

TABLE OF CONTENTS

FOREWORD

From the earliest research on Attachment Theory beginning in the late 1950s with Harry Harlow to much more recent empirical data regarding "attachment to God," the importance of developing strong attachments (i.e., intimacy) to God and others is found to be the basis of physical, emotional, cognitive and spiritual health.

In his excellent work, *The Eternal Bond*, David English gives not only sound biblical insight but carries it through to sound practical application that can transform lives and relationships. David shows that the concepts of boundaries and bonding are not antithetical, as it might seem at first glance. He shows the importance of what a Christ-follower needs to focus on (bonding) and to protect (boundaries) in order to find one's purpose.

The need for a work of this kind at this time in the Christian community is clear. Christians are immersed in a culture that denies the reality of a metanarrative, a grand story in which to integrate our personal narratives, our personal stories, our personal lives and relationships. It is this metanarrative that gives our lives purpose, and the grand story can only be discovered in truth when we are in a personal relationship with the God in whom we are to "live, move and have our being." We are not left adrift on a sea of relativity, but we have a compass, a map, which directs our lives toward the grand story and our part in it.

Throughout the history of the Church, God has raised up individuals with an ability to not only find their own way but with a gift to act as a mentor and guide to others. It is out of David's own life story, his purpose in mentoring and guiding others to find the grand story and their role in it, that David English offers this text.

I am one person who has been touched by David's call to mentor and guide others. As a young man recently graduated from college, David challenged me with investing my life in the Great Commission and making disciples. It was an important time in my life and it profoundly changed my life forever.

Even to this day, several decades later, I see my role as a professor and dean at a Christian university to be part of the grand story to make disciples that are touching other lives with the love and message of Jesus Christ.

If you are a person seeking greater intimacy with God, or even if the concept seems to be somewhat frightening, I encourage you to take a step of faith and immerse yourself in the offerings of *The Eternal Bond*.

Even better, I encourage you to get in a group with other Christ-followers and move to a new level of understanding and application by using the helpful discussion questions found in the text. In so doing, I believe you will cultivate new dimensions in your intimacy with God and others that will lead you to greater clarity in God's purpose for your life.

Gene A. Sale, Ed.D.
Dean, School of Education
and Behavioral Studies

Palm Beach Atlantic University
West Palm Beach, Florida

My prayer for you
is that God through the
power of the Holy Spirit
will transform your person
through the bond
you experience
in Him.

*…that He would grant you,
according to the riches of His glory, to be
strengthened with power through His Spirit in the
inner man, so that Christ may dwell in your hearts
through faith; and that you, being rooted and
grounded in love, may be able to comprehend with
all the saints what is the breadth and length and
height and depth, and to know the love of Christ
which surpasses knowledge, that you may be
filled up to all the fullness of God.*

Ephesians 3:16-19

Preface

God's design for His creation of us has always been for the purpose of us experiencing deep bonding with Him and Him experiencing deep bonding with us. Nothing brings Him greater joy and pleasure than that we would be one with Him in our person. Being one with Him is the greatest joy and pleasure that we could ever experience. I say this not in a superficial way, or attempting to be overly spiritual. It is the greatest reality of our lives that the God who created the universe desires that we experience an intimate, deep, bonding, lifelong, eternal relationship with Him.

I had been a Christian for 23 years and in full-time Christian ministry for 20 years before I awakened to the fact God has a much deeper priority for my life than service for Him. His purpose and highest priority for me is to experience the grace gift of relationship with Him. And the depth of that experience with Him is not reserved for the future when I will be with Him in heaven where there is no sin, but is graciously to be experienced today in a world that is wicked, perverse, and dominated by sin.

God is gentle, humble, and my soul finds rest in Him in a world that is dominating, controlling, manipulating, and willful. The desire of my heart is for His person to be reflected in me. Integrity of person, godly character, and my life lived every day in the context of deep relationship with God are high values to Him and to me. The values of the world are a polarity. The kingdom of heaven and the world cannot be mixed together. The world offers us works, performance, striving for perfection, entitlement, and obligation. Our life will only make sense emotionally when it is lived in the reality of God's kingdom of grace, relationship, beauty, and truth.

My experiencing intimacy with God is still growing. Every day I am learning how to relate better to God who is always available to fully relate to me. The joy and pleasure of the last 20 years of relationship with God could be compared to nothing else. Christ has become my life and He alone is my righteousness. It is His grace that always astounds me and binds me to Him.

It was never my intention to write a book. The relational intimacy of the Kingdom of Heaven can only be passed on to others through relational intimacy. Being bonded to God and experiencing intimacy with Him is not a formula, strategy, discipline, or a book to be read. An intimate kingdom cannot be experienced in non-intimate ways. Being bonded to God is learned from those who have deep bonding with God as the purpose of their lives. Bonding is taught and caught. But without the teacher experiencing God as the purpose of life, it is simply information to be communicated, a study to be accomplished, or a good book to be read. It is relationship that transforms, not information.

However, as I have worked with small groups of men, they have desired more than just the outlines of the material I have shared. Both men and women have encouraged me to put the truths I have experienced in writing so that they could further study and better communicate these truths themselves. Many times after sharing with a group I would think of a point that I wished I would have remembered and had failed to communicate. It has been my desire to gather the thoughts, illustrations, scriptures, and personal examples together so that I could be a more effective communicator. And so I have written this book.

Deep bonding and relationship with God does not take place without deep bonding and relationship with a few others in our life. I call these covenant relationships of the same gender. These covenant relationships work best when a small group (3-5) get together 2-3 times a year for at least an overnight and process life together, both personally and spiritually. There are also kingdom citizen relationships that are one-on-one times that are weekly opportunities to authentically share with another our life experiences with the theme always being "intimacy with God is the purpose of life."

My burden has been for men to experience deep intimacy with God and that has been the focus of the ministry God has given me for which I have desired to be an intimate steward. My vision is that God would raise up a worldwide relational network of covenant teams and kingdom-citizen relationships of men who want to grow personally and spiritually for a lifetime in intimacy with God and in deep bonding with each other. All of these truths in *The Eternal Bond* can be applied to women. In my writing I have not intended for it to be exclusive for men but to be inclusive of women also.

My intimacy with God is greatly as a result of my wife, Beth. It was she who awakened me in a kind, gentle way to the fact that I was not living the priorities I desired for my life. What I was doing in ministry had become a greater priority than the relational value base God had given me. I had developed an unhealthy sense of drivenness to prove who I was by what I did. Even though I was involved in Christian ministry full-time, the accomplishment and fulfillment of strategy and tactics had become a refuge for my lack of intimacy with God and others. Over the years, Beth has affirmed me and been my companion as I have sought to be a companion to God. She understands and experiences intimacy with God in a deeper way than I do. As we experience oneness with God and each other, I have learned so much from her. She truly is a grace gift from God to me. I dedicate my writing of this book to her.

My prayer for you as you study *The Eternal Bond* is that God through the power of the Holy Spirit will transform your person through the bond you experience in Him.

David A. English

God intended
a special place for us
to know and experience Him,
resulting in grace gifts
of protection and
provision.

Then the Lord God took the man
and put him into the garden of Eden
to cultivate it and keep it.

Genesis 2:15

Introduction

It was new and beautiful. Nothing had ever been created before that was like it. There was now a place where God could relate to and fully experience His creation of mankind. God called it the Garden of Eden. He placed Adam in His garden and gave him a tour of it so that he could see how magnificent it was. It was a place where the trees and vegetation were pleasant to see with plenty of food that was desirable and good to eat.

There are two references to the creation of the Garden of Eden in the biblical account in Genesis:

> *"And the Lord God planted a garden in the east, in Eden; and there He placed the man whom He had formed."* Genesis 2:8

> *"Then the Lord God took the man and put him into the garden of Eden to cultivate it and keep it."* Genesis 2:15

The term garden in the Hebrew language refers to a walled enclosure. It is a parcel of land that has geographic boundaries defined by walls. The walls could have been of stones, mud bricks, or hedges. They could have been of thick vegetation, mounds of earth, or thickets of thorns. We don't know for sure what composed the wall but it gave definition to the area of the garden. Adam knew where the garden existed and where the garden ended. There was not a middle ground where he could be partially in the garden and partially outside of it. He was placed by God in the garden and what was within the walls of the garden were established by the boundary.

There was a boundary that allowed the garden to be a place of protection and provision. The wall of boundary allowed the garden to be a place where provision for man was given as a result of the grace of God and protection for man was also given as a result of the grace of God.

Eden is a Hebrew term that refers to great joy, delight, and pleasure. That was the purpose of the Garden of Eden. It was a place where God and man experienced great joy and pleasure in intimacy of relationship with each other. That bonding, abiding, oneness of person was the intention of God for the creation of mankind.

Adam and Eve were created in God's image and according to His likeness (Genesis 1:26). They reflected the attributes of God in their person. God's attributes of love, justice, kindness, and goodness could be reflected in their lives through godly character so that love, justice, kindness, and goodness could be characteristic of their person. Reflecting God was not a work to be performed but the result of a relationship that was experienced. The healthy boundary established around the garden was the knowing and experiencing of God as an intimate relationship and not a work to be performed. The boundary of the garden allowed grace and relationship to be safe. There was no opportunity for works and performance to, in any possible way, be exchanged for the relationship priority of the Garden of Eden.

The result of knowing and experiencing God through His graceful provision and protection is great joy and pleasure. They can be experienced only through Him. The greatest demonstration of grace is the gift of relationship with God. And Adam and Eve experienced that gift of relationship with God from the beginning of their creation. All they experienced was a grace gift from God: relationship, beauty, food, work in the garden, and exercising great care over the garden.

Adam and Eve lived their total existence in the grace gift of relationship with God. Everything in the context of the garden was always related to their relationship with God. There was no context for which they lived and experienced life other that the deep, intimate, bonded, relationship they had with God. He was their all, their life. They walked with Him, talked with Him, labored as one with Him, and cultivated the boundary of intimacy with Him as the purpose of life.

The care and growth of the garden was a responsibility given to Adam. He was to cultivate the garden (Genesis 2:15). It involved labor and toil that was needed in order for the garden to grow and reproduce. I'm sure it involved labor that any gardener or farmer would be familiar with today. The land was to be tilled, planted, and watered. There was pruning and harvesting that was needed.

There was the cultivation of a portion of land that Adam was given as a specific responsibility. But the cultivation of the land was to be done in the context of the intimacy of relationship with God and the intimate stewardship of oneness with God in the responsibility that Adam had been given. He was not on his own to cultivate the garden but all of his labor was in the context of himself and God. He trusted in, relied upon, drew strength from, and was completely dependent upon laboring with God as one with Him as opposed to a responsibility that he had been given that he had to fulfill on his own.

This was a critical relationship to be reckoned. Work is to be accomplished in the context of intimacy with God. We tend to view vocation as separated from our spiritual lives. Nothing could be further from the truth when examining the first man and the work he was given.

There was a responsibility of cultivation of the garden but there was a responsibility of greater priority to cultivate relationship with God. And this bond between God and man (as the purpose of the creation of man) involved the cultivation of relationship – God with man and man with God. The role of work was not to separate God and man but to draw them more deeply together as one. Work was only one of many responsibilities that God gave man (cultivate and keep the garden, rule over all fish, birds, and animals, nourish oneness with Eve…) that were of lesser priority than intimacy of relationship with God.

Adam was also given the responsibility to keep the garden (Genesis 2:15). Keep means he was to preserve, maintain, watch over, and defend the garden. It means to place a hedge around. The term garden refers to a walled enclosure. We examined earlier the uncertainty as to the nature of the construction of the wall of the Garden of Eden. However, the physical plot of land had a wall around it that served as a protection for the trees and vegetation. The boundary kept the good things of the garden that brought nourishment and growth to it on the inside and the things that would bring harm and destruction were kept outside of it. It was a boundary that Adam was to watch over and maintain. That boundary was necessary in order for the garden to grow and flourish.

God had created the garden with a boundary that enabled His intention for the creation of man for intimacy with Him to be established and defended. The responsibilities He gave to Adam were to have boundaries around them so that there would be a protection of the priority of relationship between God and man and the priority of work as an intimate stewardship of oneness with God and man. Adam had the responsibility to honor and maintain those boundaries.

There are four boundaries that God desires for us to keep that ensure that we are cultivating relationship with Him:

- The Priority Boundary of Intimacy of Relationship

- The Boundary of Oneness As Mission

- The Boundary of Intimate Stewardship of Resources

- The Crucial Boundary of Rest

As we keep these boundaries, we cultivate the eternal bond we have with God. Life, in its essence, is relational. These boundaries are protections God has given us to help us value relationship over performance. They keep us from the comparison and competition of life that goes beyond the reasonableness of good stewardship. These boundaries help us to "go for it" in work, ministry, and life without developing an unhealthy sense of drivenness to prove who we are by what we do.

But most of all, these boundaries help us to truly know and experience God and to have healthy, bonded covenant relationships with others.

The world (outside of the garden) has different values and priorities that are polarities of the Kingdom of God. Some of these values and priorities are:

- Power and Domination Over Others, Where Personal and Vocational Needs Are Met, Focus On a Life of Worldly Success

- Performance Is the Road to Success and It Happens Through Hard Work

- Losers Are Those Who Can't Compete Because They Prioritize Relationships Over Accomplishments

- Relationships Exist to Meet Personal and Vocational Needs

- Relationship Intimacy Should Be Avoided Because It Is Not Safe to Truly Be Known

In the world, there are no boundaries. There are no absolutes. Performance is never fully satisfying because there is always more that needs to be done in order to prove one's worth through accomplishment. Behavior is not based upon relationship with God (godly character) and so it is a free for all – anything goes. Comparison, competition, performance, and appearance are the economy of the world. Life is lived for self, the pace is fast, and there is not time or priority for meaningful relationship with God and others. Truth is a preference that leads to deception rather than a direction that builds godly character that gives stability. Work is accomplished through drivenness that ultimately is not satisfying rather than grace relationships experienced with God and others that bring great satisfaction and pleasure. Beauty is a distortion that must be owned instead of valued and appreciated. Light (revealing what is hidden) is to be avoided because there is no safety in full disclosure of who we are rather than walking in the light of being fully known by God and a few others. Life is to be achieved by one's own best efforts (looking out for number one) as opposed to real life experienced through service and sacrifice for God and others.

And ultimately being a world dweller results in a life of frustration, bitterness, and disappointment. We can deceive our mind to believe that all the world has to offer will be satisfying, but we cannot fool our soul. Apart from the deep, relational bonding experienced with God, life will not emotionally make sense.

We were created to be citizens of the Kingdom of God with relationship with God as the purpose and priority of our existence. The world cannot and does not understand and relate to this. Relational intimacy with God is foolishness to the world.

But to the kingdom citizen, who has experienced a lifetime of deep intimacy with God, there is great joy and pleasure in life that cannot be experienced in the world.

Christ's joy was a
relational glory that He had
with His Father.
No matter what the agony,
no matter what the circumstance,
His joy and pleasure in life was the
intimacy of relationship
He had with His Father
that was the purpose
of His existence.

The glory which You have given Me
I have given to them, that they may be one,
just as We are one; I in them and You in Me,
that they may be perfected in unity, so that the world
may know that You sent Me, and loved them,
even as You have loved Me.

John 17:22-23

THE BOUNDARY OF INTIMACY WITH GOD AS THE PURPOSE OF LIFE

I. A Kingdom of Relationship and the World of Performance

Adam and Eve lived in relational intimacy with God. But the intimacy was broken when sin entered the world through their act of disobedience toward God in eating the forbidden fruit. God drove them out of the Garden of Eden, and they entered the world.

Adam and Eve had to cultivate relationship with God and keep the boundaries necessary for relationship in a much more difficult environment called the world.

Their relationship could not be restored through any works they could perform. God would provide a future way for them to be restored but that restoration to be provided from God could not be on the basis of any work or performance on the part of Adam and Eve or their future generations. They could experience relationship again on the basis of their faith in believing that God would make a future provision for their sin. But relationship and performance are polarities. Relationship cannot be received or experienced on the basis of works / performance.

We face these same two realities daily: the Kingdom of Heaven and the world. Both are inescapable. Intimacy with God can only be experienced in the Kingdom of Heaven. When we look at the boundary of intimacy with God as the purpose of life, we must examine the influence that the world exerts upon us. The world is the opposite of and in opposition to the Kingdom of Heaven. They don't mix together.

Let's take a look at how they function and the differences between the two.

The Kingdom of Heaven

The Kingdom of Heaven is a relational kingdom, an intimate kingdom, and a spiritual kingdom. It is an unseen kingdom that is more real than the world which is seen. It is the Kingdom of God and the realm where we experience Him.

In the Kingdom of Heaven you experience relationship with God, grace, beauty, and truth. It is an everlasting kingdom with light and life. Let's take a look at some of the attributes of God, which comprise some of the realities of the Kingdom of Heaven where we experience the Eternal Bond with God.

The Kingdom of Heaven and the World Are Opposites (Polarities)

Grace   Relationship   Truth   Life   Light   Beauty   Bonding

Relationship with God is the shared glory of the kingdom.

Matthew 13 refers to the Kingdom of Heaven many times in parables. It is described in verses 24-30 as **wheat sown by the servants and tares sown by the enemy**. Wheat is the grain that will provide food and the tares are the weeds that have grown up with the wheat. At harvest time, the tares are gathered first and burned and the wheat is then gathered and stored in the master's barn. It is further explained (verses 36-43) that Christ is the sower of the seed and the field is the world. Satan is the sower of the tares. The wheat are the sons of the kingdom and the tares are the sons of the evil one. There will be a future separation of those who are wheat and those who are tares. The wheat will be with God eternally and the tares will experience eternal separation. The Kingdom of Heaven is an eternal relationship experienced through the righteousness of God in Christ.

It is compared in verses 32-33 to a **mustard seed** (the smallest of seeds) that is planted and grows into a tree that shelters birds. Relationship with God starts small but grows, nurtures, and provides great enjoyment.

Verse 34 refers to the kingdom as **leaven** that allows bread to rise. Leaven is special because it gives bread its texture and size. Relationship with God is special because it gives our person life and satisfaction.

It is a joyful, relational kingdom. It is compared in verse 44 to a **hidden treasure** in a field that a man finds and sells all that he has to buy the field. The joy of relationship is far greater than anything that can be possessed.

A costly pearl, of great value, found by a merchant seeking pearls, is described in verses 45-46. For those who seek the kingdom, they find it of greater value than anything else and give up all for it. Relationship with God is the purpose and highest value of life.

It is also referred to as a **dragnet** used in fishing. The net is cast into the sea and gathers all kinds of fish. The good and the bad fish are separated. The good fish have an eternal relationship with God, and the bad fish experience eternal separation from God. The Kingdom of God is an eternal bond of relationship with God.

A relational Kingdom of God has relational qualities. It is everlasting (eternal), nurturing, special, of great joy and pleasure, and of high value.

Grace is the gift of relationship with God. It is an unmerited, undeserved gift. Grace is how the Kingdom of God functions. Grace gifts and not performance is the economy of the Kingdom of Heaven.

Ephesians 2:8-9 speaks of salvation as by grace through faith, and not on the basis of works.

> *"For by grace you have been saved through faith; and that not of yourselves, it is the gift of God; not as a result of works, so that no one may boast."*

Our growth in Christ or sanctification is also through grace.

> *"Therefore as you received Christ Jesus the Lord,
> so walk in Him."* Colossians 2:6

We receive Christ by grace through faith. And we walk or grow in Him by grace through faith. Works is not the way in which spiritual growth takes place.

Grace gifts (God giving and us receiving, and us giving and God receiving) are the ways we experience the Kingdom of Heaven. All of life (our circumstances, our relationships, our difficulties, our joys) is filtered through the prism of God's grace. Our responsibility is to bond with Him in deep intimacy, and He transforms our person to be like Him as we experience Him. Grace is the economy of the Kingdom of Heaven that makes results gifts from God and not as a result of works we perform.

Another characteristic of the Kingdom of Heaven is **beauty**. There is physical, observable beauty. When I look at a sunset on a cloudy day there is a breathtaking beauty to that event. There are multiple, complex things that are happening in order for us to experience the beauty of the sunset. It only happens when the sun is at a particular setting in the sky. The clouds have a density and a location that are favorable. The horizon is observable. And there are many other contributing factors. All of these factors and conditions, in the right timing at the right locations, create a beautiful sunset. It is a complex happening.

A bird soaring in the air, a magnificent sculpture, the leaves of trees in autumn, or a rock-bedded rippling creek in the mountains, all speak to us of beauty and complexity.

They also speak to us of relationship with God, the Creator. The complexity of the beauty of creation is like the complexity of relationship. Personal relationships have many aspects and nuances to them. As individuals, we are multifaceted in our perspectives, values, and backgrounds. When we relate to another person, there is the blending of our person with their person that mixes all of these personal complexities together. Relationships are intricate with many parts to them. But that also produces a relational wonder and beauty that is like the wonder and beauty of a sunset.

The Kingdom of Heaven is a kingdom of beauty. It is the physical, observable beauty of God's creation that reflects the relational beauty of knowing and experiencing God, who is beauty.

Truth is a value of the Kingdom of Heaven. It is the foundation for life. It is the absolute reality, which forms the basis for our views and judgments. Truth can be counted upon. It doesn't change with circumstances or situations. It is absolute and not relative. It is factual and certain. It, too, is relational.

God is truth. Jesus referred to Himself as the way, the truth, and the life (John 14:6). He is the reality of the factual foundation for life. The attribute of truth is an aspect of His person and experienced and known by us when we are intimately connected to him.

Truth is beautiful. It is wonderful. It gives us stability and security. It is an unchanging reality. It is in a relationship with God that we experience Him as truth; and He gives stability, objectivity, and integrity to our person.

The Kingdom of Heaven also has the characteristic of **light**. The purpose of light is to disclose the things that are hidden or not visible because of darkness. It illuminates and brings brightness and gives clarity. Light gives brilliance to the Kingdom of Heaven.

Jesus referred to Himself as the Light:

> *"I am the Light of the world; he who follows Me will not walk in darkness, but will have the Light of life."* John 8:12

> *"This is the message we have heard from Him and announce to you, that God is Light, and in Him there is no darkness at all."*
> 1 John 1:5

> *"In Him was life, and the life was the Light of men. The Light shines in the darkness, and the darkness did not comprehend it."*
> John 1:4-5

The relational Kingdom of Heaven is where God, who is the light, reveals or discloses Himself to us. He does not hide or withhold anything about Himself from us. He is brilliance that illuminates life.

Life is found in the Kingdom of Heaven. Life in the kingdom is not a physical existence. It is a quality experience. We all have descriptions of what life is like for us. For some, it can be boring and uninteresting. It can be disappointing and painful. For others, it can be pleasant and enjoyable. More excellent, greater, and exceeding are synonyms for abundant. Life in the Kingdom of Heaven is abundant and meaningful.

There are three words for life that are used in the New Testament: *bios*, *psuche*, and *zoe*. *Bios* is used in reference to physical life. It has a beginning and an ending. *Psuche* refers to life as individual and unique. Personality is a good way to express *psuche*. *Zoe* refers to a quality experience of life. It is the term that is always used in the context of life found in God. It is the life that is found in His kingdom. Jesus said,

> *"The thief comes only to steal and kill and destroy; I came that they may have life, and have it abundantly."* John 10:10

Life in the kingdom is not dependent upon circumstances. It is not related to working hard to find happiness. It is relational life that is experienced through intimacy with God.

The Kingdom of Heaven is an **eternal bond** that we experience with God. The emphasis here is upon a relationship that has no ending. The world will pass away. There is an eternal separation from God. But there is the eternal, everlasting Kingdom of Heaven where experience with God has no end. It continues on after physical death.

> *"Your kingdom is an everlasting kingdom, and Your dominion endures throughout all generations."* Psalm 145:13

> *"For God so loved the world, that He gave His only begotten Son, that whoever believes in Him shall not perish, but have eternal life."* John 3:16

> *"This is eternal life, that they may know You, the only true God, and Jesus Christ whom You have sent."* John 17:3

Bonding describes the relationship we experience with God. It is the eternal life relationship of oneness we have in God. Acts 17:28a puts it this way,

> *"for in Him we live and move and exist...."*

It is an eternal, everlasting bond that is the purpose of God's creation of us.

Being a citizen of the Kingdom of Heaven is experienced through knowing God personally through Jesus Christ. It is a relationship that transcends our physical life. It has a beginning (when we accept Christ for the forgiveness of our sins), but it is a relationship that has no ending.

The World

The world is the second reality we face daily. It is the opposite of the Kingdom of Heaven. It is the visible and material. Its existence is temporary. It is the kingdom of Satan, who is the enemy of God.

The Kingdom of Heaven and the world are polarities:

relationship / performance
grace / works – obligation
truth / deception – perversion
light / darkness
beauty / distortion
life / death
bonding / isolation

The Kingdom of Heaven and the World Are Opposites (Polarities)

Grace	Relationship	Truth	Life	Light	Beauty	Bonding

Works	Performance	Deception	Death	Darkness	Distortion	Isolation

Look at Appendix 1 for further contrasts between the Kingdom of Heaven and the world.

Let's look at some of the characteristics of the world.

The world is the realm of **performance**. Accomplishment is the highest value in the world. Comparison and competition are the mediums in which performance is elevated. Rivalries exist to equal or surpass another in competition.

Works are the way in which the comparisons are judged.

Domination, control, and manipulation are all related to performance. These are the behaviors in which we attempt to get our way. The end result of high performance, in which we get our way, is power. Power over others is a major goal communicated in the world. We work hard to become powerful.

The world is all about self; self-interests, self-fulfillment, personal affluence, and individual power. Recognition, position, competency, and wealth are ways that the world communicates value. In and of themselves these things are not necessarily without merit. However, they are insufficient when tied to power as the goal of life. When our identity is in the world then performance will direct our person to a drivenness that can never be satisfied. There will always be goals that hold only temporary satisfaction. Even if we were to accomplish our goals, self always craves more.

The Kingdom of Heaven and the world are polarities: grace / works – obligation, relationship / performance, truth / deception – perversion, light / darkness, beauty / distortion, life / death, and bonding / isolation.

In my book, *Banners of Bonding*, the Kingdom of Shere is compared to the world:

> The lower level reality is a material reality. It relates to the physical, material world. It is the reality of what is seen, can be touched, and experienced physically. There are no absolutes in the lower reality because truth is preferential. It is the realm of darkness. The lower level reality is governed through willfulness. Domination, control, and manipulation are the methods of willful authority. The lower reality is the natural realm.
>
> It is a realm of works and performance. Obligation and entitlement are ways in which work is performed. Taking is a result of this realm. It is a realm of simplicity because you work to produce a result. Self-effort is the key to experiencing the lower level reality. It is a sphere where there are no boundaries and integrity is not valued. Competence and effectiveness are the values of this reality. What you accomplish is more important than who you are. Behavior is a free for all that is accentuated by perversion. The focus of this reality is upon self. The lower level reality is called the world.
>
> The book of Ecclesiastes refers to the lower level reality of the world as "under the sun." This phrase is used more than 30 times

in Ecclesiastes and is best expressed in the term vanity. Why do the wicked seem to prosper and the righteous suffer? Why does one person toil endlessly and see little results when another with casual effort sees great return? In the place of justice there is wickedness and in the place of righteousness there is wickedness.

Laboring in the world to find fulfillment in the pursuit of pleasure only brings futility.

> *"All that my eyes desired I did not refuse them. I did not withhold my heart from any pleasure, for my heart was pleased because of all my labor and this was my reward for all my labor. Thus I considered all my activities which my hands had done and the labor which I exerted, and behold all was vanity and striving after wind and there was no profit under the sun."*
>   Ecclesiastes 2:10-11

Ecclesiastes describes the world as wearisome, striving after the wind, and futility. Other terms that are used are vexation, foolishness, and folly.

The world seems to make sense but its reality is one of death not life. To try to link one's life to the pursuit of all the world offers will only end in frustration.

But we have to live in the world and to an extent we have to accommodate the lower level reality. We have to make a living and our income is generally determined by how hard we work to earn a wage. Performance becomes an indicator of financial success. There is a government we live under and laws that govern us. At times, we will have to relate to the world; but we cannot allow the world to preside over us. The world may seem to make sense in our mind, but it will never emotionally make sense in our heart.

Discussion Questions

1. What do you feel are the greatest contrasts between the Kingdom of Heaven and the world?

2. In what areas of your life do you find the lure of the world most compelling?

3. What motivates you the most to seek first God's kingdom and His righteousness (Matthew 6:33)?

II. God Values Relationship Over Performance

My brother, John, and his wife, Melanie, were with Beth and me as we sat in the waiting room of the hospital. My father, Eugene English, had been diagnosed with colon cancer and was being operated upon. Four years earlier, he had heart bypass surgery. My mother, Martha, had passed away three years earlier from peritoneal cancer after an operation, chemotherapy, remission, and a reoccurrence of the cancer.

I wasn't doing well in the hospital waiting room. Emotionally, I considered what it would be like to be without my father. Apart from my wife, Beth, my father was my best friend. I didn't want to think of him as being in pain or dying.

The doctor came out and shared that it was a successful operation. He felt that the tumor was removed but that dad would need chemotherapy to be sure that all traces of the cancer would be eradicated.

As Beth and I returned to our home in Northwest Arkansas, I shared with her that I didn't know how much longer my dad would live. I felt that I wanted to spend intentional time with him in the future so that we could be together more often, experiencing each other. He was such a joy and pleasure to be with.

After thinking about it for several months, I had this bright idea!

My dad attended the University of Oklahoma (OU), and that was also where I graduated from college. Our daughter, Christa, was going to be a freshman there in the fall. Why not purchase some season football tickets and spend the weekends of the home games with him at his home and then go to the games together? He only lived about an hour from Norman, Oklahoma and dad loved OU football.

I applied for five season tickets and, to my surprise, was able to get them; and they were pretty good seats. The Sooners hadn't done well in quite a few years, and so it was relatively easy to obtain tickets. And, after all, my goal was to be able to spend time with dad, and this gave us the opportunity to do so. Beth was able to come, and we brought our children also. It was a family thing – to be with papa for the weekend!

That first year of home games with dad was delightful, even though the Sooners didn't do well on the field. Dad was finishing his chemotherapy; and, even though he was weakened physically, our times together were emotional highs for all of us.

The Sooners began to improve; and in 2000, we observed an undefeated season and a national championship. We certainly had a lot more enthusiasm and excitement about the team when they were winning. Being able to high five each other and hug after touchdowns were more commonplace than in the previous years. But what was more exciting than winning was that I was able to be with my dad and enjoy him.

In the summer of 2006, dad was diagnosed with congestive heart failure. Each game that fall I could visibly notice his increasing lack of strength. It was becoming more and more difficult for him to walk the half-mile to the stadium and to climb the stairs to our seats. Even sitting the length of the game became a very tiring experience for him.

It was at the ending of the last home game of the season that dad asked me to walk down the stadium stairs in front of him so that he could put his hands on my shoulders to steady himself as he walked down. I knew then that this was the last game my father would ever attend. He died a month later.

In Hebrews 12:1-2, life is described as a race.

> *"Therefore, since we have so great a cloud of witnesses surrounding us, let us also lay aside every encumbrance and the sin which so easily entangles us, and let us run with endurance the race that is set before us, fixing our eyes upon Jesus, the author and perfecter of faith, who for the joy set before Him endured the cross, despising the shame, and has sat down at the right hand of the throne of God."*

The New Testament was originally written in the Greek language. The Greek word that is used for race in this passage is *agon*. It is the root from which we derive the English word agony. Life is an agony. There is an agony of life that God sets before us. And we are to run that race (agony) with endurance, making sure that our eyes are fixed upon Jesus. He was joyous in the midst of His agony; and that helped Him to deal with His disappointments, discouragements, and ultimately His death upon the cross.

Christ's joy was a relational glory that he had with His Father. No matter what the agony, no matter what the circumstance, His joy and pleasure in life was the intimacy of relationship He had with His Father that was the purpose of His existence. The oneness of person, no matter what the circumstance, was the greatest joy that He could ever experience. There is a relational joy in the intimate bond of oneness with God that far exceeds any accomplishment or performance that we could ever obtain.

In the midst of the anguish and agony of my life, I have a tendency to gravitate toward my performance in order to be approved and loved.

- Am I winning or am I losing?

- What do I need to do differently in order to perform better?

- How can I overcome the obstacles facing me?

- How can I become the best?

If I could pull back the curtain of life, that is so greatly influenced by the world, and receive a glimpse of God in the midst of the race He has given me to run, He would be encouraging and affirming me in what is most important to Him.

- I love you whether you are winning or losing.

- I desire relationship with you, not perfection from you.

- I am not trying to fix you.

- The character of your person is more important to Me than the competency of what you do.

- Who you are in intimacy with Me is of far greater value to Me than any position to which you might attain, any scope of responsibility that you could be given, or any task that you might ever perform.

- Who you are is more important to Me than what you do.

- My greatest joy and pleasure is to experience who you are as we walk together through the great adventure of life that I share with you.

Intimacy with God is the purpose of life. We were uniquely designed by God to be deeply bonded to Him – our person bonded to His person, His person bonded to our person.

It's like being with my father in the stands of Oklahoma Memorial Stadium. The great joy in being at the game is that I am there with him and we are enjoying being together experiencing each other.

Being with Dad and experiencing him was a far greater value than the end result of the competition on the field.

III. Descriptions of Intimacy with God

In the beginning of the Old Testament is the story of creation. God (as the Trinity) is involved in the amazing task of creating the heavens and the earth. All the galaxies, the solar systems, every star, and planet were created by Him. The world and all it contains: land, waters, vegetation, and living creatures were brought into existence by Him. Then He created mankind,

> *"Then God said, 'Let Us make man in Our image, according to Our likeness.'"* Genesis 1:26a

God created humanity as **special** to Him. When we look at all of God's creation on the third, fourth, and fifth day, they were summed up by the phrase, "and God saw that it was good." His summation of the creation of mankind on the sixth day was, "And God saw all that He had made, and behold, and it was very good."

His act of creation on the sixth day as compared to the other days of creation is explained through the term "very." Synonyms for very are incredibly, exceptionally, and extraordinarily. Looking at these words, I feel that "special" is the term I would use to contrast the "good creation" and the "very good creation."

We are special to God because we were created by Him as separate and distinct from all of His creation.

There were significant differences in the creation of mankind from the rest of His creation. Mankind was also **unique**. Humanity was unlike any other creation. There was a distinctive aspect to man that could not be duplicated or even have any resemblance to the rest of creation. Uniqueness also meant that in future generations of mankind each individual would be unique. No two human beings of God's creation of and reproduction of mankind would be the same.

My brother and I look alike. We have a similar physical inheritance from our parents. However, we are both unique. I have a friend that when he has an appointment tells people whom he has never met that they will recognize him because he looks like Abraham Lincoln. And he does! But he is not Abe Lincoln. He only has a resemblance to him.

Whether it is physical distinctions, personal temperaments, or behaviors we have, there may be people of similarities but every person is unique.

God created all of humanity of **high value to Him**. This is communicated when God says that He created us in His image according to His likeness. Nothing else in all of creation is like the nature of God. Mankind alone reflects who He is and is according to His likeness. He values humanity more than anything else outside of the Trinity.

When I am with my children at school events, they are the ones upon whom my attention is centered. Whether it is band, football, swimming, or academics, my focus and my heart is with them. They are of higher value to me than the other children, teachers, the activity in which they are participating, or the school itself.

God's heart, His attention and His concern is with humanity, which He created. And all of humanity is of high value to Him.

All of humanity is unique, special, and of high value to God because they are His creation. Uniqueness, specialness, and high valuableness are not based upon our performance. They are not based upon experienced relationship with God. Mankind is unique, special, and of high value to God whether or not they experience relationship with Him. Those who are far from God, who have no interest in Him, or who may even be antagonistic toward Him are still unique, and special, and of high value to Him.

Ephesians 2:10 uses the word workmanship to describe the special, unique, creation of high value that we are to God.

> *"For we are His workmanship, created in Christ Jesus for good works, which God prepared beforehand that we would walk in them."*

Prior to this in Ephesians 2:8-9, there is the emphasis upon the eternal life relationship with God that we can experience through grace. There is no work or merit that we could deserve or earn that would give us forgiveness of our sin. Only Christ can forgive our sin.

The focus in verse 10 is then upon the term workmanship. A better translation of the word is masterpiece. Mankind is His masterpiece creation. We are a masterpiece created by God. It refers to the special, unique, creation of high value that we are to God.

Experiencing the specialness, uniqueness, and high valuableness we are to God can only happen when we are intimately connected to Him. This takes place through establishing relationship with Him and growing in intimacy with Him. The nature of our creation is to experience God. Intimate experience with God is the purpose of life.

Our desire to live a life of separateness apart from God is an inherited spiritual condition of our lives. It is what the Bible refers to as sin. It can be acts of outward rebellion toward God or simply passive acts of indifference toward Him.

> *"For all have sinned and fall short of the glory of God."*
> Romans 3:23

> *"For the wages of sin is death, but the free gift of God is eternal life in Christ Jesus our Lord."* Romans 6:23

God gives us the opportunity for our sin to be forgiven, to establish relationship with Him, to experience intimacy with Him, and to experience how we are unique, special, and of high value to Him as His creation. It is through the acceptance of Jesus Christ for the forgiveness of our sin that we are able to know and experience God. Otherwise, we will experience a life of separation from Him and miss the life of great joy and pleasure that can only be found in Him. The unique, special, person of high value to God that we were created to be will live life in isolation from God (who is our Creator) seeking worth, value, and significance apart from God. The abundant life, found only in intimacy with God, will become elusive and self-focused, as if we were emotionally robbed of the deep satisfaction we relationally desire.

I grew up always going to church and youth group. My father was the Sunday School Superintendent, and we were in church as a family every Sunday. It was a social time for me, not necessarily a spiritual time.

I did work hard at trying to be good and do good, but God seemed distant most of the time.

When I went to college, I occasionally attended church. It was more out of a duty or obligation that I felt.

One evening in my sophomore year, some men came into my fraternity house, had dinner with us, and made an announcement about a meeting that they were having in the living room after dinner. They said that they wanted to talk with us not about religion, or any specific denomination, but about the person of Christ and how He related to our lives as college students. I, like most of the men in the house, stayed afterward to hear what they had to say.

They talked about God's love and forgiveness, the abundant life Christ offered, and how a person could establish a relationship with Christ. Afterward I talked with one of the men about several questions I had. He was helpful; and, as I left the meeting, I knew there was a decision facing me concerning my spiritual life. I could not get to sleep that evening because I didn't know if I really knew God or not. Jesus said in John 10:10b,

"I came that they may have life, and have it abundantly."

I knew I wasn't experiencing the abundant life in Christ that they talked about. One of the verses they shared was Revelation 3:20 where Christ says,

"Behold, I stand at the door and knock; if anyone hears My voice and opens the door, I will come in to him and will dine with him, and he with Me."

That evening I decided to open the door of my life to Christ and invite Him to come in, to forgive my sins, and to show me the abundant life that He had promised. I prayed a prayer something like this:

"Lord Jesus, I need You. I open the door of my life and receive You as my Savior and Lord. Thank You for dying on the cross to forgive my sins. Show me the abundant life that You promised me. Amen."

Nothing dramatically happened that evening or the next day. I got involved in a Bible study and over time I began to see my life change. It was a transformation that was happening, not because I was working hard outwardly to change my life, but because God was changing me from within.

As I have grown in Him over the years, I am experiencing the unique, special, person of high value to Him that He created me to be. The intimacy that He desires for me is now a realization that brings great joy and pleasure to Him and to me.

If you have never experienced intimacy with God or don't know whether you have ever established a relationship with Him, you can do so right now through prayer. You can pray a prayer similar to the one I prayed years ago when I was in college. Let me share it again with you:

> "Lord Jesus, I need You. I open the door of my life and receive You as my Savior and Lord. Thank You for dying on the cross to forgive my sins. Show me the abundant life that You promised me. Amen."

If this prayer expresses the desire of your heart, I want to encourage you to pray it now wherever you are.

If you have prayed this prayer, then certain things are now true in your life:

- You have established relationship with God through the forgiveness of your sins (John 3:16, 2 Corinthians 5:21).

- Christ is in your life (Revelation 3:20, John 17:22).

- You will begin to experience the transformation of your life (2 Corinthians 5:17).

- You will begin to experience the abundant life for which God created you (John 10:10).

And you will begin to experience a relational intimacy with God that will partly be characterized by the unique, special, person of high value that you are to Him. You were created for the destiny of your person to be bonded in this intimacy with God. There is no greater experience in life than knowing God for who He is and experiencing who He created you to be in Him.

To Be Like Him and Experience Him – Godly Character

We have already examined the first mention of the creation of mankind in the Bible in Genesis 1:26. It was in reference to the special, unique, creation that is of high value to God that is found in His creation of mankind. I want us to further examine this scripture and how it refers to the creation of mankind (our creation) and how we are to be a reflection of who He is. Let's look at two specific aspects of intimacy that are emphasized.

> *"Then God said, 'Let Us make man in Our image, according to Our likeness.'"* Genesis 1:26a

The Trinity was involved together in the creation of mankind. "Our," in the phrase, "Our image," refers to a plural rather than a singular image. There is togetherness in who they are and oneness in what they do. They participated together in the creation.

The word "man" that is used is not gender specific. It refers to all of mankind – all of humanity – men and women.

When we describe who God is, we refer to the nature of His person through His attributes. Attributes describe the nature of God. Some of His attributes are love, justice, goodness, and faithfulness. He is also kindness, grace, humility, caring, and much more. It isn't that He just acts in these ways but these are attributes of His person. He is the personification of love, justice, goodness, caring, etc. God always acts consistently according to His person, His attributes.

The word image means a reflection, resemblance, similarity, or a reproduction. We are to be a reflection of His person – His attributes. There is fullness, completion, and absoluteness in the person of God. We cannot be God in the fullness or exactness of His person. But He created us to be like Him in our person. We can be a reflection or a reproduction of Him.

If you were standing outside on a clear day, your physical person would cast a shadow. If you were standing outside with several of your friends and looking at your shadows, you could recognize each other by the differences in your shadows. Your shadow would be a reflection of your physical person but not an exactness of your physical person. In a similar way, our person can be a reflection of the person of God. We will never be an exactness of who He is but we can be a reflection of Him.

His attributes, reflected in our person, are called godly character. We can reflect His love, faithfulness, justice, and goodness. However, we cannot reflect His attributes simply by working hard to do so. He is who He is, not by working hard to do so. It is the nature of His person – His attributes – that reflect His actions. Likewise, we cannot try to act like Him and assume that we will be like Him. Our person reflecting His person only happens when we are deeply bonded in intimacy with Him. His person then transforms our person to be like Him. Intimate relationship allows us to reflect Him. The result of intimate relationship is godly character. The purpose of our creation is to be a person of godly character.

The result that God desires in relationship with us is to simply experience us as His creation. Character is the result of the bonded relationship with God. Character doesn't happen quickly. It involves bonded relationship over time. Character is the authentication of deep bonding with God. It is the result of the power of the Holy Spirit within us to transform us to become like Christ because of the abiding we have in Him.

Character is important to God. It is more important to Him than competencies we have at what we do. It is more import to God than any outcome or results that we could produce. The greatest competency that we could develop is intimacy with God.

Godly character is proof of the competency of intimacy with God.

However, there is a second aspect of a relational intimacy from this passage. We are also created "according to His likeness." This is the relationship that Adam and Eve experienced in the Garden of Eden prior to the fall (their sin). They walked and talked with God. All of who they were and all of what they did were always in the context of God. Their lives were lived in deep intimacy with God and total dependency upon Him. Their identity was bonded to God as the people that He had created them to be. There was no separation of their lives from the life that God had for them. The phrase in Genesis 1:26b, "according to His likeness," is life lived always in the context of intimacy with God.

Genesis 1:26b is a theological basis for intimacy with God through the reflection of His image and being according to His likeness. A biblical illustration of "according to His likeness" can be found in Genesis 2:7.

"Then the Lord God formed man of dust from the ground, and breathed into his nostrils the breath of life; and man became a living being."

There are several actions that take place in this passage – formed from dust, life breathed into nostrils, and becoming a living being. It is a picture of the creation of mankind in the person of Adam, the first man.

God formed him from the dust of the ground. He was physically created from the ground. God breathed into His nostrils, life, so that the physical body now was alive. Man becoming a living being is different from the creation of a physical body of which God also created a live person.

"A living being" refers to a living person that has his being bonded with the person and being of God. Adam's life was lived in the context of himself as the creation and God as his creator. There was not life apart from God. He lived the totality of his life in the context of deep relational intimacy with God.

"According to His likeness" refers to a life that is always lived in the context of relational intimacy with God.

What then is the purpose of our creation? It is to be like Him and to experience Him. That can be said in many different ways, but it is the purpose, priority, and essence of why God created us. It is a relational intimacy whose deepest experience can be found only in God.

Abiding in Him

In John 15:5, Jesus gives us another expression of what it is to have intimacy with God as the purpose of life. This passage is near the end of Jesus' earthly existence. He is comforting His disciples concerning His future departure from them. In John 15:5, He uses an horticultural illustration of the relationship that He experiences with them.

"I am the vine, you are the branches; he who abides in Me, and I in him, he bears much fruit; for apart from Me you can do nothing."

A branch grows as a part of a vine. But it is a special relationship where the branch becomes like the vine. The branch becomes like the vine because it abides in the vine. To abide is to be completely dependent upon. Remain, dwell, continue are uses of abide in the Bible.

Last year, we experienced a severe ice storm in the middle of winter. We have a little over half an acre of land where our house is located with many trees on the property. Some of our trees were severely damaged. Almost every large tree had to have broken limbs trimmed from them and some larger trees had to be removed because the damage to them was so great. Nine months later, there are trees that have recovered but a few of them still have broken branches in them that we failed to have removed. The proof of a living tree is the bearing of leaves. The broken branches have no life in them. Leaves will not grow on them. The branches no longer have a growing connection to the trees.

They are not abiding. They no longer experience a vital life-giving connection.

When we abide in Christ, we live a life of total dependency upon Him. He is our strength, comfort, sufficiency, and hope. Our life is one of never leaving Him but always remaining in Him. He is in us and His life is one of always remaining in us. He will not leave us. He will not forsake us. He is always leading, guiding, strengthening, and comforting us. When we abide in Him and Him in us, we produce fruit. The fruit of abiding in Christ is godly character.

Trees were created to bear leaves. Fruit trees were created to bear fruit. We were created to abide in Christ and be like Him in godly character and reproduce after our own kind in helping others to know Christ and abide in Him. Like leaves on a beautiful tree that characterize the tree as vital and alive, so godly character is the evidence of a life that is vital and alive in Christ. I believe that it is also the reproduction of others coming to know Christ and abiding in Him.

Fruit on an apple tree is not produced through the tree straining to do so. Apples are the natural result of a healthy apple tree. A healthy tree is the result of water, nutrients from the soil, lack of infection, and sunlight.

A grower nourishes the tree in order to have a healthy crop. It is not an automatic process. There are many factors that are unable to be controlled by the grower. When there is a healthy crop, any results are grace gifts from God. The responsibility of the grower is to nourish growth.

Our responsibility for spiritual growth is to abide in Christ who is the creator of our life. God is the initiator and grower of life. He is constantly nourishing us in intimacy with Him. Abiding means that we choose to be dependent upon Him, remain in Him, and never leave or forsake Him. When we abide, we experience Him and He experiences us.

Abiding in Christ is the purpose of life. It is the intimacy of relationship that we share with God.

Being One with Him

Just before Jesus experiences His betrayal by Judas, He has a conversation with God in which He expresses His deep desire for His disciples to be one with Him and each other like He and God the Father experience in oneness with each other.

> *"The glory which You have given Me I have given to them, that*
> *they may be one, just as We are one; I in them and You in Me,*
> *that they may be perfected in unity, so that the world may know*
> *that You sent Me, and loved them, even as You have loved Me."*
> John 17:22-23

Oneness is a description of relational intimacy. It is a shared relational glory that the Trinity has with each other. It is the priority of their existence. They will never allow anything to come between the oneness they have with each other. They are three in person and in roles but they are one in relational intimacy with each other.

One with each other is also described as the relationship that Adam and Eve were to experience.

> *"For this reason a man shall leave his father and his mother, and*
> *be joined to his wife; and they shall become one flesh."*
> Genesis 2:24

There is a leaving and cleaving in relationship with a man and a woman that should be characterized by the two becoming one.

There is a great book written by Don Meredith that describes the marriage relationship as *Two Becoming One*. In marriage, there is a separateness of person but there is also a relational oneness.

God created Adam and Eve with separateness apart from Him. They were like Him but also they were created as distinct from Him. God could have created them without separateness from Him so that they would always do what He desired for them. But He created them with separateness from Him and choice as to whether or not to pursue Him. This was risky, but God knew that He could not have relationship with them apart from it being their choice.

We cannot have a relationship with someone who tries to dominate, control, or manipulate us. They will not allow us to be a person separate and apart from them. Relationship with them only takes place when we do what they want. Power cannot make love and authentic relationship happen.

If God had not created Adam and Eve without separateness involving choice, then they would be like robots always doing His will. He could dominate, control, and manipulate them to get His way. But God is not harsh, dominating, controlling, or manipulating. God is not willful. He is humble, gentle, gracious, and restful. He does not apply force or pressure to get His way.

His desire is that we take the separateness of person that He has designed us to be and that we bring ourselves to Him to be one with Him. He created us to bring our separateness into oneness or togetherness with Him.

Relational intimacy is the glory of oneness that we have with God and that He has with us.

There was time in my life when direction, circumstances, and relationships were controlled by me. I worked hard at trying to be happy and produce good outcomes. Sometimes it seemed that life went well, but there were other times when life was disappointing. It seemed as if I was locked into producing a life that would bring success and happiness. There came a point where I became fed up with trying to make life work well through my own efforts.

Now, when I come to difficult times in my life where it seems a decision needs to be made about what to do, I want to be one with God. My desire is to not move apart from our movement together. Leaning to my own understanding and perspectives is insufficient. Many times I find myself praying: "God I want to be one with You in this. I don't want to deter one step from what You have for me."

There is great joy and pleasure in oneness with God because we are together. It is a relational glory that can be called intimacy.

Intimacy with Him

He was a lawyer who paid close attention to specifics of the law. He was well-suited for his profession because he enjoyed debating what was right and wrong. The technical points of the Roman law were his expertise. Jewish religious law was what governed his personal life and actions. Right-standing with God was important to him, and he worked very hard to follow the detailed Law of the Prophets. The Torah (the additions by the Scribes and Pharisees to the law) was something in which he was well read.

He had listened to the conversation that his friends, the Pharisees, were having with Jesus. It was a confrontational discussion, and he had a question which he asked,

> "*Teacher, which is the great commandment in the Law?*"
> Matthew 22:36

And Jesus replied,

> "'*You shall love the Lord your God with all your heart, and with all your soul, and with all your mind.' This is the great and foremost commandment.*" Matthew 22:37-38

Jesus gave the lawyer (and the other Pharisees that were listening) an answer that was difficult for him to comprehend. His life and the lives of the Pharisees were based upon the law. Performing well, the works of the Jewish law, was what to them, determined a relationship with God. The most religious people were the ones who worked the hardest at trying to perfectly perform the law. Relationship with God was not personal. It involved performance, and the standard was perfection.

Spirituality, to the Pharisees, was works to be performed, not a relationship to be experienced with God.

Jesus said the greatest commandment was a relationship with God. It was a love relationship with God that involved one's heart, soul, and mind. The heart, soul, and mind are a description of the totality of a person. And the totality of a person bonded in a love relationship with the totality of the person of God is a description of intimacy. And the greatest commandment was a definition of intimacy with God.

The purpose of life, intimacy with God, can be described in many ways; to be like Him and to experience Him, abide in Him, oneness with Him, and intimacy with Him.

Intimacy is relational and transformational. Intimacy is not about performance or works we do in order to experience relationship. It is about a relationship we experience through grace (a gift not based upon works or performance) where we are transformed (changed) because of the relationship.

Definition of Intimacy

We have looked at several illustrations of intimacy. I would like for us to now examine a relational definition of intimacy.

The tendency is to describe intimacy by the actions that are necessary for its cultivation: prayer, Bible study, fellowship with other Christians, helping those who are poor or marginalized, and communicating Christ to those who don't know Him. All of these are good practices that help us to know and experience God better.

However, actions that help cultivate an intimate relationship with God can easily become works, duties, and obligations to be done in order to know and experience God more fully. How can good actions that help develop intimate relationship become works to accomplish intimacy or duties to perform in order to experience intimacy with God? It can happen easily when we try to experience an intimate Kingdom of God in non-intimate ways.

In the Preface, I share my own personal story about the first 20 years of my vocation not truly reflecting my relational value base (God, Beth, our children, and my covenant friendships) even though I was involved in full-time Christian work. Performance and position vocationally had, over time, become a greater priority to me than relationships. As I mentioned before, I had developed an unhealthy sense of drivenness to prove who I was by what I accomplished. I was still doing the activities of relationship with God but there was the lack of intimate bonding with God. The activities had become works to perform in order to stay connected to God rather than relational ways to experience Him. They had also become duties to be performed in order to be blessed by God personally and in service I did for Him.

Sin is always trying to make relationship into a performance.

Intimacy with God can't simply be measured by the amount of time we have in Bible study and prayer. Fellowship with like-minded Christian friends is also not a determination of relational intimacy with God. Sharing our faith with others who don't know Christ and serving those who are poor or marginalized aren't necessarily indicators that we are abiding in Christ.

Intimacy can be best defined not through activities that are beneficial to it. These actions can also be detrimental when they lack heart, soul, and mind bonding with God. How do we define intimacy with God in ways that are relational? In ways that do not or cannot become performance?

We looked earlier at heart, soul, and mind when we were examining illustrations of intimacy. The passage in Matthew 22:37-38 is the key passage.

> *"'You shall love the Lord your God with all your heart, and*
> *with all your soul, and with all your mind.' This is the great and*
> *foremost commandment."*

Let's examine this passage in more detail.

The context of the passage is about a love relationship with God.
The Greek word used here for love is *agape*. It is God's love. A major
characteristic of His love is that it is unconditional. His love is not based
upon our performance for Him, neither it is based upon our acceptance
of Him. His love is a grace gift from Him to all humanity. He loves His
creation (mankind) not because they do anything for Him but because of
His creation of them.

We can only experience the love God has for us when we have a
relationship with Him through Christ's death on the cross for us. God loves
all of humanity, but only those who choose to know God by receiving
the grace gift of forgiveness of sin through faith in Christ will be able to
experience God's love.

God loves us for who we are and not for what we do for Him.

When it says, "you shall love the Lord your God," the word translated for
love is *agape*. We are to love God with the love that He has for us. We are
to love God unconditionally. We love Him not because of things He does
for us but because He is God. Our love for Him is not performance-based.
It is relationship-experienced.

We should love God for who He is and not for what He does for us.

When we can have a relationship with God that is bonded to His person
as God not because of what we want Him to do for us, and He can have a
relationship with us not based on how we perform for Him, then it is truly
a love relationship. This love relationship forms the context through which
intimacy can be cultivated.

When we look at loving God with all our heart, there are several thoughts
that come to mind. Our heart, in a spiritual sense, is not an organ that
pumps blood through our body. It is the seat of our emotions. The heart is

where adventure is found. It is where our passions reside. What we weep about (or pound the table concerning) comes from our heart. The things that empower our person come from the heart.

A great role of the heart is about that to which we surrender our lives. Proverbs 4:23 says,

> *"Watch over your heart with all diligence,*
> *For from it flow the springs of life."*

Life emotion comes from the heart – for good or for bad. Therefore, we should be careful about that to which our heart is surrendered for it will have great effect over us.

When we "love the Lord with all our heart," it means that our heart is fully surrendered to God. It is bonding our heart to His heart and allowing Him to empower our lives.

Loving the Lord with our soul is different than loving Him with our heart. Our soul is what governs our person. It is where our values and worth reside. Our soul relates to our identity or who we perceive ourselves to be.

Identity can be determined in five ways: self, others, the world, religion and God.

Many people spend a lifetime in a self-directed search to find out who they are. The result of this quest is saddening because we were not created as people of independent self-will or self-determination. We are created as beings to be connected to the Creator. He created us, not us creating ourselves.

How others perceive us and communicate to us who we should be can be a major determination of our identity. We tend to believe the opinions of others about us as truth and live our lives seeking their approval. When we do so, our identity is based upon our performance for others in order to gain their favor. This type of behavior is very defeating and produces a weariness in our soul for which we are never able to find satisfaction.

The world is constantly telling us what our personal values should be and how we should act. These voices come to us in many ways. The entertainment industry and educational institutions are constantly sending messages to us about how we should think, what we should wear, and how we should act. They try to mold the culture in their own image and are constantly marketing to find converts to their way of life. But we know the world is constantly changing, and new voices appear on the scene with ever-changing messages to mold our identity around their values. It is exhausting to keep our soul continually aligned upon a need for approval in appearance, thoughts, and behaviors.

All world religions (except for Christianity) are based on good works to be performed in order to experience relationship with their god. Religion becomes rules and regulations to be followed and behaviors to be maintained. Self-righteousness is cultivated when a person feels that they are following the rules and behaviors. Their identity is rooted in what they do to become pleasing to their god, but they always fall short of the perfection necessary in order to experience a god that is holy and perfect.

Our identity established in Christ is where true identity is found. It is not based upon self-perception, opinions of others, what the world says, or works that we perform. It is based upon what God (who created us) says is true of us as His creation. Our identity is bonded to our creator and His purpose for us. In the book, *Search for Significance*, it clearly communicates how God views us. God says,

> "You are deeply loved,
> Completely accepted,
> Totally forgiven.
> I am for you, not against you."

God speaks to our soul about His view of our value, worth, and identity. When our soul is bonded to His soul, it means that we believe who He says that we are. We don't believe what our feelings tell us about ourselves. We don't accept how we perceive ourselves. We don't listen to the hurtful perceptions from others about us. The identity the world wants us to experience is rejected by us. Working hard to be religious to gain acceptance by God is not an option we entertain.

Our true identity is that we are deeply loved, completely accepted and totally forgiven. God is for us, not against us.

Our mind is where competencies are found. Competencies are the unique, special creation we are by God. They are related to how we think, process, and work out applications of life. They are gifts, skills, and abilities that God has given us. Truth is processed in our mind. Beauty enters our person through our mind.

Direction is a key aspect of our mind. Our mind gives direction to our person. When our mind is bonded to the mind of God, then we are united in where He desires for us to go. We want to be one with Him and go in the direction that He is leading. Intimacy with God in our mind is "to be His companion and go in the direction that He is going."

I believe the best definition of relational intimacy with God comes from the understanding of heart-to-heart, soul-to-soul, mind-to-mind bonding of God and me. It looks like this;

- Surrendering my heart fully to God every hour, day, month, year – for a lifetime.

- Believing who God says that I am (deeply loved, completely accepted, totally forgiven. God is for me, not against me).

- Being Christ's companion and going in the direction He is going.

That is intimate relationship with God – heart, soul, and mind.

Discussion Questions

1. Describe in your own words what it is to have an intimate relationship
with God.

2. What results have you seen in your life as a result of intimacy with God?

IV. Sin Tries to Make Relationship into a Performance

The major effect of sin upon our person is that it tries to make relationship into a performance. Relationship with God has no attachment to works, obligation, or performance. Personal relationship with God is devoid of domination, control, or manipulation.

God is not trying to fix us so that we can act better in order to experience Him. He looks upon the attitude of our heart, which is the door that opens intimacy with Him, not the perfection of our actions.

Earlier we looked at the example of the Pharisees in Matthew 22 that is the contrast of the performance of the law to the bond of relationship. The Pharisees were a religious Jewish sect that believed that performance of the law was the basis of spirituality. When asked by the Pharisees,

> *"Teacher, which is the greatest commandment in the Law?"* Jesus replied, *"You shall love the Lord your God with all your heart, and with all your soul, and with all your mind."*

Spirituality, to Jesus, was a relationship to be experienced, not rules to be performed. It was relationship that involved the totality of a person – heart, soul, and mind – fully surrendered to the heart, soul, and mind of God.

God doesn't care about our good works, our performance to be perfect, or what we can do to attain a relationship with Him. Relationship does not come through self-efforts or personal accomplishments. It doesn't matter how good we are or how much we have accomplished.

Relationship is not a performance. The intimate kingdom of Heaven is about grace and relationship. The world is about works, obligation, and performance. And sin is always trying to make relationship into a performance.

When sin entered the world, there were personal and relational effects that took place. The wonderful environment to experience God in the Garden of Eden was no longer an option for Adam and Eve. Relationship had to now be experienced in the context of the world. There was now an environment in which they lived that was contrary to and always in opposition to relationship with God. It was the environment of the world, and it is the same opposition that we experience today.

Sin tries to make relationship into a performance in personal and relational ways.

There are three predominate personal effects of sin: isolation from God, independent spirit of self-will, and focus upon self (rather than God and others).

When Adam and Eve sinned, they hid themselves from God.

> *"They heard the sound of the Lord God walking in the garden in the cool of the day, and the man and his wife hid themselves from the presence of the Lord God among the trees of the garden."* Genesis 3:8

Adam and Eve no longer experienced the deep intimate relationship that they previously had with God. Rather than deep bonding with God, they were experiencing separation from Him. They weren't seeking God, but instead were hiding from Him. Sin causes us to emotionally isolate ourselves from God and from others.

Adam had also developed an independent spirit of self-will about his life. Rather than seeking to experience the relationship he previously had with God of completely living his life in the context of God, he chose to go his own way, apart from God. He lied about his condition rather than being honest with God.

> *Then the Lord God called to the man, and said to him, "Where are you?" He said, "I heard the sound of You in the garden, and I was afraid because I was naked; so I hid myself."*
>
> *And He said, "Who told you that you were naked? Have you eaten from the tree of which I commanded you not to eat?"*
>
> *The man said, "The woman whom You gave to be with me, she gave me from the tree, and I ate."* Genesis 3:9-12

Adam blamed Eve and God (the woman You gave to me) for his sin. Rather than relating to God, he acted independently from God. That independent spirit of self-will, apart from God, determining one's own destiny is a personal effect of sin that all mankind has inherited.

The third personal effect of sin is to be self-focused rather than focused on God and others. The living of life in the context of relationship, the oneness and abiding relationally with God, has now been replaced with a focus upon self.

It is the theme of the last verse of the poem *Invictus* by William Ernest Henley:

> It matters not how straight the gait,
> How charged with punishments the scroll,
> I am the master of my fate;
> I am the captain of my soul.

Being the "master of my fate and the captain of my soul" is a good description of many people that I know. Some wander through life aimlessly seeking to find who they are and to discover their destiny in life. Others charge through life seizing the opportunities available to promote self and prove who they are by what they do. No matter what path they pursue, there is an emotional restlessness within them that will never be satisfied apart from intimacy with God. Just because sin entered the world, it did not change the original intention of God's creation of us – to experience intimacy with Him.

There are three predominate relational effects of sin: separation in relationship with God, personal relationship confusion about one's identity, and confusion in relationships with others.

There is an endowment, which God gives all mankind. It is the desire for intimacy with Him. This relational oneness with God has been placed within the heart of all humanity. But not everyone responds to the desire to know and experience God.

Saint Augustine said, "Thou has created us for Thyself O God, and our hearts are restless until they find their rest in Thee."

Blaise Pascal, French mathematician, physicist, and philosopher, put it this way, "There is a God-shaped vacuum in the heart of every man that can be filled by no created thing except by God, the Creator, made known through Jesus Christ."

We were created to experience intimacy with God, but sin separates us from Him and causes us to minimize the priority of relationship with Him.

Sin also confuses us about our own identity. In our intimate relationship with God, our identity is who we are as His created being. We are special, unique, and of high value to God. We looked earlier at our identity described as deeply loved, completely accepted, and totally forgiven by God. He is for us – not against us. It is the value base out of which the soul of our person can be anchored.

Let's look again at some of the ways in which our identity is determined. Sin confuses us to think that our identity can be found in self. It is a lifetime search to discover who we are. Sin also confuses us to think that others can determine our identity. Their approval and acceptance cause us to have to perform for them in order to be someone of value to them. When we give in to others determining our identity, we disrespect our person who is created in the image of God.

The world can also try to give us its values as our identity. When that happens, we become involved in a comparison and competition with others in which behavior becomes a free for all. There are no absolutes and the world is like a magnet – always drawing us away from a relationship with God-based identity. And we can also allow religion (performance-based spirituality) to determine who we are through good works.

We can fool our mind as to how we determine identity. But our soul, emotionally, will only experience true satisfaction when our identity is grounded in intimacy with God, and we believe who He says that we are as His creation.

Sin is constantly at work confusing us relationally as to our value and worth and how they are determined by God and experienced in relational intimacy with Him.

Sin also affects our relationships with others. We play games relationally by trying to dominate and manipulate to get our way. We deceive so that we can control relational outcomes. Comparison and competition with others can become a way of life in order to appear that we are valuable and worthy.

Relationships can be dominated by performance. The world's perspective of honesty, vulnerability, and humility become the characteristics of a loser rather than the signs of godly character.

Sin damages us personally and relationally, but it need not be so. Intimacy with God as the purpose of life is the bond that is relational and transformational. He will transform us to be like Him when we are one with Him, abiding in Him.

Just because sin entered the world, it did not change God's original intention for us to experience intimacy with Him as the purpose of our life.

Discussion Questions

1. In what ways do you find yourself performing for God in order to gain
   His approval or receive things from Him?

2. When do you find yourself most isolated from God? How does isolation
   cause you to feel and act?

V. Covenant Relationships with Peers Are Essential to Experiencing Intimacy with God

God did not create us to fully experience intimacy with Him in a relationship of just us and Him. He gives us other special relationships in life in which we relate to them in the way we relate to God. These are a handful of people who are grace gifts to us from God. I call these special relationships covenant relationships.

There are four kinds of covenant relationships:

- God to His people.
- A husband and a wife.
- A parent to a child.
- Close friends of the same gender.

We have previously looked at God's covenant relationship to His people. The basis for it is His creation of us and our acceptance of His provision for our sin in Jesus Christ. When we fully surrender our person to Him, then we are able to experience His person bonded to our person. Our surrender brings great joy and pleasure to God because He is able to experience intimacy with us. That intimacy is the purpose of His creation of us.

God also gives us other people with whom we can experience intimacy. We relate to them in the ways God relates to us – we love them for who they are and not for what they do for us, we accept them as a grace gift from God, we respect their person even when they say no to us, we serve and minister to them, we put boundaries together around anything that prevents intimacy with God, and we are one with each other in pursuing intimacy with God as the goal of life.

Husbands and wives see their covenant relationship with God and with each other as the foundation of their marriage. They love each other unconditionally, sacrifice for each other, and powerfully serve each other.

Children are unable to experience covenant relationship with their parents, but parents can do so toward their children. This is called a unilateral covenant. It is a covenant to relate to their children in the ways in which God relates to them.

Covenant relationships of the same gender are essential to experiencing intimacy with God. These relationships are more than good friendships. *Forsaking All Others* explains that covenant relationships with peers of the same gender are characterized by certain criteria:

- Christ as Our Life
- Confidentiality
- Authenticity
- Availability
- Mutual Respect
- Focus on God and Others (Transcend Self)

The design criteria for a team of covenant relationships of the same gender is three fold:

- They focus upon intimacy with God and bonding with each other.
- They are intentional in being together.
- They are not planning on the relationships ending.

Some key verses that describe covenant relationships of the same gender are:

"A man of too many friends comes to ruin, but there is a friend who sticks closer than a brother." Proverbs 18:24

"Iron sharpens iron, so one man sharpens another."
Proverbs 27:17

"A friend loves at all times, and a brother is born for adversity."
Proverbs 17:17

There are three major benefits of covenant relationships with the same gender:

- They help us experience deeper intimacy with God because they relate to us the way God does.
- They help us to grow in godly character.
- They help us to live a lifetime of faith in Christ.

As we look at the cultivation of intimacy with God and the boundary of the purpose of life as intimacy with God, it will not happen without others of the same gender with whom we experience covenant relationships.

In my experience, covenant relationships of the same gender take two practical forms: **covenant teams** and **kingdom-citizen relationships**. They both have the same criteria, design principles, and benefits that we looked at earlier. However, they differ in three areas; size, age proximity, and meeting frequency.

	Covenant Team	**Kingdom Relationship**
Size	3-5 people	one-on-one
Age Proximity	peers of similar age (similar phase of life)	can be different ages (different phases of life)
Meeting Frequency	2-3 times a year for at least an overnight	meet weekly

We have to be intentional in seeking out and developing covenant relationships. Very rarely will these bonds with another develop without us taking the initiative to pursue others with whom we feel a covenant relationship could develop. Check out Appendix 2 for more detailed input on how to develop a covenant team of peers. My friend, Alan Wagner, developed distinctives of covenant relationships (team of peers or kingdom-citizen relationships). Look at Appendix 3 for what they are and what they aren't.

As I meet with my covenant team and those with whom I have covenant relationships, there are four principles that help us to stay focused on intimacy with God as the purpose of life:

- Character is more important than competency.

- Godliness is more significant than giftedness.

- Depth of intimacy with Christ is of far greater value than any position, scope of responsibility, or task that you could ever perform.

- Who you are is more important than what you do.

Intimacy with God is the purpose of life. Relationship with God is cultivated and not a formula that we accomplish. As we live our lives, we must always keep the boundary of intimacy with God as the purpose of life. Our true identity cannot be separated from God's created identity for us. Life only emotionally makes sense when we have fully surrendered our life to God. Any other purpose in life will be insufficient and will result in a dissatisfaction characterized by "life seeming to not make sense emotionally."

These truths and others need to be processed in our lives through covenant relationships with others who desire to love God with all of their heart, soul, and mind. This bond we have with others is crucial to fully experiencing God. It is His design for deep intimacy with Him to take place as a result of deep bonding and intimacy that we experience with others. Without these covenant relationships, our bonding with God is difficult because we do not experience the reality of Him in our daily life with others. When others are at a distance emotionally and relationally from us, we miss the opportunity for oneness with them. That separateness from them may seem safe and keep us from the pain of their suffering and hardship, but Christ enters into our pain and hardship. He suffers with us through His suffering that He endures and comforts us with Himself. He takes our experiences in life and identifies with them and walks through them with us. He does not distance Himself from us in order to escape our pain, nor does He leave us on our own to fend for ourselves. He desires that we abide together and are one with each other. This intimacy with Him is the purpose of life. No matter what we experience, He is one with us and we are one with Him. Our life is hidden in Christ with God.

His design is that the oneness that we experience with Him will manifest itself in oneness with certain people with whom He has graced us. We have to be intentional in pursuing these covenant relationships with others.

Covenant relationships with others are essential to intimacy with God.

Discussion Questions

1. Who are your closest friends and how did they become so?

2. Why do you feel that covenant relationships with peers of the same gender are essential to your covenant relationship with God?

3. If you presently don't have covenant-relationship friends, what are the next best steps that you would take to develop these relationships?

VI. God Gives Us a Voice

As we grow in intimacy with God, over time, there are great truths we learn about God and about ourselves. We discover areas of our lives in which we have strengths. They give us great satisfaction when we are able to exercise them. There will be areas in which we are not gifted and lack competencies in execution.

There will also be spiritual areas of our lives in which we will grow and learn for a lifetime. Some spiritual truths are lessons that come easily, but others are harder to learn. God's grace is experienced as abundant in the lessons that are enjoyable. At the times of hardship and suffering, it is a grace that is sufficient. Being a follower of Christ isn't an entitled path of assurance that we will not have difficulties. Annie Johnson Flint wrote a poem that I memorized as a new Christian that speaks to these issues.

> God hath not promised skies always blue,
> Flower-strewn pathways all our lives through;
> God hath not promised sun without rain,
> Joy without sorrow, peace without pain.
>
> But God hath promised strength for the day,
> Rest for the labor, light for the way,
> Grace for the trials, help from above,
> Unfailing sympathy, undying love.

As we walk with God through all of life – the pain and the hardships, the abundance and the blessings – God promises us Himself. He journeys with us and discloses to us who He is as God. And a special grace gift He gives us is a voice from Him.

Let's look more at this voice He gives us.

The World Has a Voice for Us

The world is the opposite of the Kingdom of Heaven. Its values have no place for God and are all about independence from God and the promotion of self. The voice of the world is about power, position, fame, and accomplishment. The focus is upon self and performance as the means to having a powerful voice. The world values what we do rather than who we are.

The voice of the world says that power, position, and wealth give us a voice. That voice will always be centered in performance and accomplishment. When the voice of the world becomes our voice, then we share how successful we are about what we have accomplished. Our voice enters a realm in which comparison, competition, and accomplishment are center stage with the voices of others who compete with us for dominance. It isn't good enough to be a mother who seeks the well-being of her child. She has to be the best mother. It's not enough to be a businessman who labors with integrity. He has to excel when compared to other businessmen. No matter what our profession or vocation, the world of comparison and competition so dominates our person that we believe that accomplishment is the identity that gives us a powerful voice.

We see and hear that voice every day, "Look at me and what I have done (or am doing)!" I am someone because of what I have accomplished. I am powerful because I have wealth. Position gives me the privilege to have others serve me in my quest for greater accomplishment. Effectiveness at competency in performance is more important than character or integrity.

When we listen to the voice of the world, we will speak to others about our wealth, power, position, and accomplishments. Our voice, from the world, may not be a loud, clanging cymbal, but, nonetheless, it comes from the values of the world that have molded our soul.

The values of the world are inappropriate voices that have influenced us away from truth and the priority of relationships. Here are a few of those voices:

- Personal peace and affluence are the keys to life.
- The end justifies the means.
- Character is not important if one is competent at accomplishment.
- Look out for number one.
- Use people for personal gain.
- If it feels good, do it.
- There are no absolutes.

In the *Introduction*, I shared about the contrast between the kingdom of God and the world. Some of these worldly values are reiterated.

The world (outside of the garden) has different values and priorities that are polarities of the kingdom of God. Some of these values and priorities are:

- Power and Domination Over Others, Where Personal and Vocational Needs Are Met, Focus On a Life of Worldly Success
- Performance Is the Road to Success, and It Happens Through Hard Work
- Losers Are Those Who Can't Compete Because They Prioritize Relationships Over Accomplishments
- Relationships Exist to Meet Personal and Vocational Needs
- Relationship Intimacy Should Be Avoided Because It Is Not Safe to Truly Be Known

In the world, there are no boundaries. There are no absolutes. Performance is never fully satisfying because there is always more that needs to be done in order to prove one's worth through accomplishment. Behavior is not based upon relationship with God (godly character), and so it is a free for all – anything goes. Comparison, competition, performance, and appearance are the economy of the world. Life is lived for self, the pace is fast, and there is no time or priority for meaningful relationship with God and others. Truth is a preference that leads to perversion rather than a direction that builds godly character that gives stability. Work is accomplished through drivenness that ultimately is not satisfying, rather than grace relationships experienced with God and others that bring great satisfaction and pleasure. Beauty is a distortion that must be owned instead of valued and appreciated. Light (revealing what is hidden) is to be avoided because there is no safety in full-disclosure of who we are, rather than walking in the light of being fully known by God and a few others. Life is to be achieved by one's own best efforts (looking out for number one) as opposed to real life experienced through service and sacrifice for God and others.

And ultimately being a world dweller results in a life of frustration, bitterness, and disappointment. We can deceive our mind to believe that all the world has to offer will be satisfying, but we cannot fool our soul. Apart from the deep, relational bonding experienced with God, life will not emotionally make sense.

We were created to be citizens of the kingdom of God with relationship with God as the purpose and priority of our existence. The world cannot and does not understand and relate to this. Relational glory in intimacy with God is foolishness to the world.

When the world gives us its voice, it will only have a temporary sound of success that relates to performance. To maintain that voice requires a lot of time and energy to continue to excel. It is a voice that becomes tiresome, frustrating, and shaming (because we can never do enough). It is a voice that will have a bitter, self-centered, wounding, and entitled sound. It isn't a pleasant voice for others to hear because it speaks of self and value that is related to performance. It is a voice that has to be maintained at the expense of personal reality and authenticity.

God Gives Us a Voice that Comes from Our Weakness

There is a tendency to think that spirituality always involves strength. We feel that we must be strong as we face the challenging circumstances of life.

We have been taught that it is our strength that defines us. The resume of who we are should not include the difficult times or the perceived failures. Our power to persevere and willful strength in the midst of hardship are how the world characterizes influential people.

It is not so in the kingdom of God! The power of God is made known within us, not through our successes and victories. He shows Himself in the greatest ways in our life, not in our "having it together" or in "our great accomplishments."

His power is demonstrated in us through our weaknesses, greatest hardships, and suffering. Paul describes this in 2 Corinthians 12:9-10.

> *And He has said to me, "My grace is sufficient for you, for power is perfected in weakness." Most gladly, therefore, I will rather boast about my weaknesses, so that the power of Christ may dwell in me.*

> *Therefore, I am well content with weaknesses, with insults, with distresses, with persecutions, with difficulties, for Christ's sake; for when I am weak, then I am strong.*

God's greatest demonstration of Himself within us coming through our weaknesses is hard to "get our minds around" because it is so contrary to the world. In the world, power is attained through position and wealth. They form a foundation that allows one to "get their way." Control, domination, manipulation, and intimidation are tools in the arsenal of power that are to be wielded, when necessary, to get what you want. To express weakness is to be considered as inferior and to be trampled upon. Hard core achievement, at the expense of covenant relationships, is what characterizes worldly success. It is an insatiable power that will consume our life demanding all of us and there is always more that will need to be accomplished.

The world will never acknowledge that life, in its essence, is relational.

Our Voice Comes from Our Intimacy with God Through His Grace that Is Sufficient

In the midst of the confusion of the world, God gives us a deep penetrating voice about Himself in which there is confidence, security, and safety. Our voice is a grace gift from Him. But it has been developed from His grace that is sufficient, not from His abundant grace. We don't have to seek the voice that God has for us. Our voice will seek us out. Our voice will find us. It will be a gift from God. Our voice will be totally contrary to the speech we will hear from the world.

I'm not talking about a spiritual message we share. Our voice is not related to a mission, vocation, or cause in which we are involved. It is very easy to confuse the voice God gives us with a mission or a destiny He has with us in what we do.

It isn't necessarily an audible voice of God speaking to us. Truth that we have or convictions that we have developed aren't the nature of our voice. It isn't a mystical or magical happening through which our life has been changed.

Our voice comes from the intimacy of relationship we have with God and what He has shown us about Himself in our greatest trial. He gives us a certainty about Himself from His attributes or His truth that will be undeniable to us, and a lifelong relational glory we will have with God. It is an aspect of who He is that will never be doubted by us and no person or circumstance can take it away from us.

Our voice is based upon the poverty of spirit we have toward God. He is our life, and we desire oneness with Him at all times. We will put boundaries around anything that would prevent intimacy with Him being the purpose of our life.

There are times when God's answer to desires that we have is a "no." In His "no's" to us, there are some that are very difficult to accept: the pain from the cancer for which there is no cure, the marriage that has not happened, the broken relationship with no reconciliation, the death of a loved one, and many other "no's" in which there is suffering and persecution. "No," from God, for many people, is a received as a being rejected by God. Relationship for them is about getting their way. If the answers to what they feel they want and need are not "yes" from God then they reject Him.

The real question we face is, "Will we continue to be one with God when the outcome is not pleasant?"

Job, probably the wealthiest man in the world in his time, lost everything. He experienced the death of family members, lost his ways of making an income, and experienced extreme health problems. Job understood that "no" from God can be an acceptable answer even though he experienced great pain and suffering. The voice that Job had was expressed through the most difficult time in his life. He walked with God through extreme hardship, pain, and suffering, and God ministered to Him through the oneness of intimacy that they shared with each other. Job's voice cried out,

"Though He slay me, yet will I hope in Him." Job 13:15

The voice God gave Job was – God can be trusted!

Another illustration of God's voice comes from the story of Joseph (Genesis 37-50).

Jacob had 12 sons of which Joseph was the youngest. Jacob loved Joseph, but his brothers hated Joseph because of the special relationship he had with his father. They plotted to put him to death and threw him into a pit. Instead of killing him, they sold Joseph to a traveling party of merchants who took him to Egypt. He was sold as a slave to Potiphar, the captain of Pharaoh's bodyguards.

Potiphar made Joseph his personal servant. As his servant, Joseph managed his household well and all of his lands. But Potiphar's wife falsely accused Joseph of having sex with her, so he was put in prison. After two yeas in prison, Joseph was called upon by Pharaoh to interpret a dream that he had. Because of the successful interpretation of his dream, the Pharaoh made him ruler over all of Egypt.

Many years later, his brothers came to Egypt during a famine seeking food. Joseph recognized his brothers but disguised himself so that he would not be recognized. He sold grain to them and even returned their money from the sale of the grain to them. They returned again for more grain, and Joseph disclosed himself to them and they reconciled themselves to him. They all, with their families and their father, moved to Egypt.

Joseph endured slavery and imprisonment unjustly. His brothers convinced his father that he was dead. Joseph was eventually positioned as the right-hand man of Pharaoh, managing all of Egypt. Yet through all of his pain, suffering, and rejection, God revealed Himself to Joseph in a special way. In Genesis 50:20, he shares,

> *"As for you, you meant evil against me, but God meant it for good in order to bring about this present result, to preserve many people alive."*

The voice God gave Joseph was,

> "God is good."

Our voice is found in the most difficult thing we have ever had to experience – the greatest suffering we have encountered – the darkest day of our life. In this time of difficulty, we have walked through it with God. We trusted Him when there was no hope. We sought intimacy with Him when emotionally there was nothing in us.

It may still be a trial or a suffering that we continue to endure. Our voice is not about "how we saw God come through." It is about experiencing Him who walks through it with us.

Our voice is the unique truth that God has given us about Himself (His attributes) that we desire for others to deeply understand and experience. Our voice has three criteria:

- The deep touch of God in my life that I have experienced through hearing His greatest "no" for me.

- The power of God impressed upon my soul that comes from my deepest weakness.

- The awesomeness of God experienced through my poverty of spirit toward Him and others.

Our voice, when given by God, will be gracious, kind, humbling, and grateful.

My friend, Steve Graves, says that many Christians have a karaoke voice. It is a voice that comes from the last Christian book they read or the last podcast to which they listened. We are familiar with people who are always sharing the voices of others with us. And every week it is a new truth from the deep experience of the hard circumstances that others have gone through and the voice that God gave them.

God uses the voices of others to encourage us and to help us to live lives of faith in God. We can rejoice in and learn from the voice that God has given others, but He has designed a voice that He desires to give to us that is something special. It is deeply relational and powerful. Our voice bonds us to God no matter what the circumstances. It is a unique voice, coming from our soul, that encourages others to more deeply seek an intimate relationship with God.

Our Voice Is Not About Our Mission

There is a great tendency to relate our voice to what we do for God and others. Mission is an outgrowth of relationship. It is a joy that we share with God. The circumstances surrounding how God gives us a voice may lead us to mission that is related to those issues. However, we must be careful to recognize that the voice God gives us speaks to our relationship with Him. God gives us His voice in mission and we will look at this later. The voice He gives us speaks of who He is in our life.

The founder of the organization I work for was Bill Bright. His mission statement for the unity of accomplishment that he so desired with God was, "The Fulfillment of the Great Commission in this Generation." He wrote of it in his books. He spoke of it whenever he was with any audience. The closing in every letter he wrote was, "Yours for fulfilling the Great Commission in this generation." It was a task to which he dedicated his life, but it was not the voice God gave him.

Dr. David Jeremiah, in the foreword to Bill Bright's book, *First Love* (written in 2002), wrote this:

> For most of my life, I have admired Bill Bright as a champion for world evangelism and Spirit-filled living. Not until I read his new book, *First Love*, did I understand completely the spiritual dynamic that has driven him for the 50 years of his ministry.

> As I read the pages of *First Love*, I realized that the highest priority of Bill Bright's life has not been Campus Crusade (Cru), or even evangelism. His first priority has been, and is today, his personal relationship with Jesus Christ.

The voice God gave him was, "Never Leave Your First Love for Christ." At every gathering of the staff of Cru, this is the message he would share. The voice God gave him was a greater priority to him than the mission God gave him.

Our Voice May Take Time and Maturity

With most people, it takes time and maturity to discover their voice. Our voice is a grace gift from God and that could be given at an early age. But for many people, hardship and suffering are experienced as they grow older. Living a life of faith in God, in the midst of difficulties, will over time help us to truly see the reality of God in our lives. He cares for us, suffers with us, endures hardships, and grieves with us in our sorrow. Christ has experienced and does presently experience our deepest trials and darkest days with us. He suffers when we suffer and experiences our pain. It is in the crucible of the weaknesses of our life experiences that we forge our deepest bonds of intimacy with Him. Those deep bonds are generally formed over time.

As I have shared earlier, one of the darkest times in my life was in my early 40s. Through caring conversations initiated by my wife, I came to realize that vocational success had become a greater priority to me than relational significance with those most dearest to me in life. I realized that I had not truly lived my life according to my priorities. An overemphasis upon success vocationally had clouded my thinking about the priority of relationships and the importance of character over competency. It wasn't that disastrous things were happening relationally or that there were deep character flaws appearing. It was that my identity was becoming linked to my professional accomplishments rather than my relationship with God and my other covenant relationships (Beth, our children, and close friendships).

Jeb Stuart Magruder, an aide to Richard Nixon and Watergate conspirator, who later became a Presbyterian minister, shared in his autobiography *From Power to Peace,*

> "I climbed to the top of the ladder of success, only to discover that the ladder was leaning against the wrong building."

I felt that same pain as I assessed my first 20 years of ministry. This was devastating to me because I had invested so much time and energy in wanting to be a success at what I did that my closest relationships in life were slighted because of my lack of care and concern for them.

I had become a workaholic who was driving down a fast lane of accomplishment. Position and responsibility were to me like alcohol is to an alcoholic. You dangle them in front of me and because of my addiction to them it was incredibly difficult for them not to control me. I had realized that personal success had become an idol in my life. The service that I was doing for God had become more important to me than my relationship with God.

As I stepped back from position and began to work responsibly in roles where I could be authentic about my priorities in life, there were truths that began to grip me:

- Never leave your first love of Christ.

- Consider all things as loss in view of the surpassing value of knowing Christ.

- The relational value base that God has given me – Beth, our children, and close covenant friends – is more important than my vocation.
- Who I am is more important than what I do.

And God gave me a voice,

"Intimacy with God is the purpose of life."

It has taken most of my life for my voice to find me. The full surrender of who I am and what I do were the criteria necessary for God to entrust my voice to me. My voice is a motivation to me every day of my life. It is like a directional North Star to which I continually align my priorities and direction. It is a grace gift from God that is humbling to me and gives me safety and security in Him. I really like to share my voice with others!

Once more, "Intimacy with God is the purpose of life!"

Discussion Questions

1. Is "God's power matured through your weakness" a reality in your life? If so, how? If not, why not?

2. Is there present suffering in your life that you must continually walk through with God? What has He shown to you about yourself in the midst of this suffering? What has He shown to you about Himself in the midst of this suffering?

3. Our voice is the unique truth that God has given us about Himself (His attributes) that we desire for others to deeply understand and experience. Our voice has three criteria:

   • The deep touch of God in my life that I have experienced through hearing His greatest "no" for me.

   • The power of God impressed upon my soul that comes from my deepest weakness.

   • The awesomeness of God experienced through my poverty of spirit toward Him and others.

Examine your thoughts about these criteria in your life. Write down the unique truth that God has given you about Himself.

God has good works for us
to fulfill in oneness with Him.
It is a mission in which we abide
in Him for what we do.

For we are His workmanship,
created in Christ Jesus for good works,
which God prepared beforehand
so that we would walk in them.

Ephesians 2:10

THE BOUNDARY OF INTIMACY AS MISSION

I. Oneness As Mission with God

In the earlier section, we talked about intimacy with God as the purpose of life. It was a boundary that will allow us to enjoy the greatest joy and pleasure that we could experience in life. It is a personal relationship boundary. It is who I am, relating to who God is; and who God is, relating to who I am. The relationship is based upon grace and cultivated through grace.

The opposite of grace is works. Works, obligation / entitlement, and performance have no place in relational intimacy. Performance is the opposite of relationship. Obligation / entitlement is the polarity of grace gifting.

God has a dream for our lives. His dream is His greatest desire for us.

God's dream for us has two aspects: a dream for our purpose and a dream for our mission. We have already examined the first aspect of the dream: the purpose of our life as intimacy with Him. The description of that purpose in Genesis 1:26 is that we would reflect His image and be according to His likeness. Reflecting His image means that we are like Him. His attributes are reflected in our person. Another way to explain that is to say that we are a person of godly character. To be according to His likeness is to experience God by living our life totally in the context of trust and dependency upon Him.

His dream is that we would be a person of godly character who lives our life in complete dependency upon Him. That was the relationship that

Adam and Eve had with God prior to their sin. Just because sin entered the world, God's dream did not change. It will always be that we experience intimacy with Him as the purpose of our life.

However, there is a second aspect to God's dream for us. It is a directional dream for what we do. It involves our destiny. I refer to it as our mission in life. Mission, not in the strict definition related to use of the word in Christian mission, but the broader use of the term as vocation or profession. It is this direction in life that involves our destiny. I refer to it as mission.

The key to understanding the mission that God has for us is that we are one with Him in what we do. Ephesians 2:10 says,

> For we are His workmanship, created in Christ Jesus for good
> works, which God prepared beforehand so that we would walk
> in them.

God has good works for us to fulfill in oneness with Him. It is a mission in which we abide in Him for what we do. A central theme of God's dream for our life in oneness of mission is that the dream will always transcend self. God did not create us to live a life focused upon self. His dream is for intimacy of oneness with Him in mission, and that involves service for and ministry to others. It is a God and others focus.

Acts chapter 14 describes Paul and Barnabas in Antioch where they had seen many become believers in Christ, and they also encouraged the churches in their faith. In verse 27, the ministry they had was described.

> When they had arrived and gathered the church together, they
> began to report all things **that God had done with them** and
> how He had opened a door of faith to the Gentiles.

This same wording is used in Acts 15:4.

> When they arrived in Jerusalem, they were received by the
> church and the apostles and the elders, and they reported all **that
> God had done with them.**

The phrase "**that God had done with them**" is another way to express intimacy as mission with God.

A similar phrasing is used in Acts 15:12.

> *All the people kept silent, and they were listening to Barnabas and Paul as they were relating what signs and wonders **God had done through them** among the Gentiles.*

God and us involved in intimacy as mission could be expressed as **what God had done with us** or **what God had done through us**. It is mission or destiny with God in what we do. It is not a separateness of what we feel we should do, hoping that God will bless what we think is best. We desire to be one with Him in what are His desires.

Here are some thoughts from *Banners of Bonding* about intimacy of oneness with God in the destiny He has for us.

> Unity is relational. It refers to unity of purpose. We have looked at ways in which this relational unity can be expressed: oneness, bonding, togetherness, abiding, and intimacy. These are all descriptions of the unity that God desires with us.

> There can also be unity of mission or accomplishment that refers to works we do. It is the unity of accomplishment that comes from the oneness, bonding, togetherness, abiding, and intimacy that we have with God.

> There is the unity of purpose with God that produces His person through our person. This is called godly character. And there is the unity of our mission with His mission for us that produces godly accomplishment. The Bible calls this good works. The key to understanding good works is that they are done in unity with God. We can do good works apart from God but we will not experience the exciting relationship of doing them in unity with God. When we do good works apart from God we also tend to take the credit for them and define our person by the works we do. We can become like the Pharisees who measured their spirituality by the things they accomplished.

> When we determine the works we do in life apart from God, then we go through life in a self-centered context. It's not worth it.

Mission in life will be truly satisfying when it is lived in the context of our life-transcending self. Peter Haile in his book, *The Difference God Makes,* puts it this way:

> "Most of us end up serving ourselves most of the time. We hear talks suggesting that we should free ourselves from responsibilities so that we can find ourselves. We hear that we should look out for number one. But life will never work properly so long as we are serving ourselves. The happiest people I know are people who have lost themselves in the service of others."

If we say that we have unity with God in our mission but make our own decisions about the direction of our life, then we are double-minded about life. We want to love God but want to serve self. In James 1:7-8, it says the double-minded man will be unstable in all his ways. Instability in life will come from self-centeredness of mission.

Life will only make sense emotionally when our purpose and mission in life are firmly established in unity with God. Unity as mission is established the same way that unity of purpose is established. It comes through complete surrender of what we desire to do unto God.

Faith is a key ingredient to be mission-centered in God. The mission that God has for mankind is the unity they can experience with Him. He loves the world and is desirous that no one would perish (or experience life apart from Him). He has a plan for the ages that is involved in the redemption of mankind unto Himself. When we have unity as mission with God, we will be involved in His plan for mankind. We will have His heart for those who don't know Him. We will be burdened for those who know Him but don't really experience unity with Him. We will desire for the unity of purpose we have with God to be experienced by all of mankind. We will want the whole world to know Him as we do. We will be involved in a mission that is spiritual that transcends our own needs. We will be involved in the unity of fulfillment of good deeds that God directs us in through the unity of our persons.

But many times the actual initiation or first-steps of accomplishing the unity of good deeds will require faith. Many times our emotions will tend to direct us toward what is comfortable and acceptable by others. Emotions make it easy to be passive and be self-centered rather than focus upon the things of God. When we trust our emotions and don't trust by faith the desire of our heart to accomplish good deeds in unity with God, then we miss the exciting adventure of life for which God created us.

When we examine mission, the Bible refers to this as stewardship. God's desire is that we have an intimate stewardship with Him. It would be the same thing as saying we that we have oneness of mission.

Paul Laurence Dunbar, in his poem *Too Busy*, expresses the struggle of doing our own thing in life or having unity with God.

> The Lord had a job for me, but I had too much to do.
> I said, "You get someone else – or wait till I get through."
> I don't know how the Lord came out, but He seemed to get along.
> But I felt kind o' sneakin' like; cause I knowed I'd done Him wrong.
>
> One day I needed the Lord, needed Him right away –
> And He never answered me at all, but I could hear Him say
> Down in my accusin' heart, "Child, I's got too much to do.
> You get somebody else, or wait till I get through."
>
> Now, when the Lord has a job for me, I never tries to shirk;
> I drops what I have on hand and does the good Lord's work;
> And my affairs can run along, or wait till I get through.
> Nobody else can do the work that God marked out for you.

Here are some verses that speak to the oneness of intimate stewardship. They have given encouragement and comfort to me as I try to keep the boundary of intimate stewardship.

> *"Trust in the LORD, and do good;*
> *Dwell in the land and cultivate faithfulness.*
> *Delight yourself in the LORD;*
> *And He will give you the desires of your heart."*
>   Psalm 37:3-4

"Trust in the LORD with all your heart.
And do not lean on your own understanding.
In all your ways acknowledge Him,
And He will make your paths straight." Proverbs 3:5-6

"For I am confident of this very thing, that He who began a
good work in you will perfect it until the day of Christ Jesus."
Philippians 1:6

"'For I know the plans that I have for you,' declares the LORD,
'plans for welfare and not for calamity to give you a future and
a hope. Then you will call upon Me and come and pray to Me,
and I will listen to you. You will seek Me and find Me when you
search for Me with all your heart.'"
Jeremiah 29:11-13

We can be involved in mission that comes from working to accomplish good deeds that are done through self-effort. It sounds ridiculous. How can what has been established and cultivated in oneness of purpose of life (intimacy with God) become a mission that outwardly seems to transcend self but in reality is all about works, performance, and self-effort? How does grace become works? Relationship become performance? Grace gifts turn into obligations / entitlements?

It can easily happen when we do not keep the boundary of intimacy as mission.

Intimacy as mission takes place when we are fully surrendered to God and trust the power of the Holy Spirit within us to accomplish God's results. The good works that God has prepared for us are not to be accomplished through self-effort. It is the Holy Spirit that empowers and transforms our person, and it is the Holy Spirit that accomplishes the destiny that God has for us. We are to trust and depend upon the Holy Spirit to empower us, and we are to be responsible to keep the boundary of intimacy as mission.

Discussion Questions

1. Describe what intimacy as mission with God looks like in your life.

2. In what ways do you presently find your life transcending self (God and others focus)?

3. How can intimacy as mission with God become an independent pursuit of one's own direction in life apart from God?

II. We Were Designed
to Dream Big

My first year in full-time Christian work, I believed that we were simply "one good rallying cry message at a fall retreat" away from worldwide evangelism. After forty five years on staff (seven of those overseas), I have learned that reaching the world with the message of God's love and forgiveness in Jesus Christ is more complex that I first envisioned.

One of my areas of struggle is with the largeness of organizational goals and my limited resources. As I develop my annual strategic plan for ministry, I desire to set realistic / faith goals. I don't want to look at comfortable, attainable goals that could happen without intimacy of stewardship with God. But I also don't want to be unrealistic and set goals beyond my faith in what God has for us. Planning and dreaming with God involves much time in seeking Him, attentively listening to Him, intelligently hearing from Him, and obeying His voice.

My organization is always setting goals way beyond the ones for which I am trusting God.

Early each Monday morning I plan my week. My desire is to relate the activities of my schedule to the goals I have for the year. Once I have the week planned, it is as if I receive a text-message from my regional team. The message is always the same, "Do more!" And after I have rearranged my schedule to accommodate more, another text-message arrives from the national team. It is always the same, "Get-r-done!"

I don't receive text-messages from my leadership that are like that. They are great people that keep the boundary of intimacy as mission with God. But I can visualize unrealistic expectations that come from others that are simply not true. Even if others were not involved I will place those expectations upon myself.

The same is true in secular vocation. Our employer has dreams for the growth of the organization. In order for it to be profitable and grow and expand, we must be employees that share in the dream for company growth. But how does that work in a practical sense where we have limited personal resources and our employer's vision is constantly expanding?

What is it to be one with God in the mission He has for me? What is the role of scope in that mission? How can I dream and plan so that I do not minimize what God has for me? How do I dream and plan so that I do not exaggerate what God has for me?

I have to acknowledge that God dreams and plans big.

Let's look at His dream and plan for mankind.

> *"The Lord is not slow about His promise, as some count slowness, but is patient toward you, not wishing for any to perish but for all to come to repentance."* 2 Peter 3:9

> *"This gospel of the kingdom shall be preached in the whole world as a testimony to all the nations, and then the end shall come."* Matthew 24:14

> *"And Jesus came up and spoke to them, saying, 'All authority has been given to Me in heaven and on earth. Go therefore and make disciples of all the nations, baptizing them in the name of the Father and the Son and the Holy Spirit, teaching them to observe all that I commanded you; and lo, I am with you always, even to the end of the age.'"* Matthew 28:18-20

> *"After these things I looked, and behold, a great multitude which no one could count, from every nation and all tribes and peoples and tongues, standing before the throne and before the Lamb, clothed in white robes, and palm branches were in their hands; and they cry out with a loud voice saying, "Salvation to our God who sits on the throne, and to the Lamb."* Revelation 7:9-10

God's desire is that all of humanity might come to know Him. His vision is for multitudes from all nations, tribes and tongues to experience eternal life that is only found in Him.

Others can dream and plan big. Earlier we examined how Bill Bright used to sign his letters, "Yours for fulfilling the Great Commission in this generation." His vision of God was large enough to encompass the world.

Steve Douglass, present Director of Cru, dreams and plans for "Movements Everywhere." The campus ministry of my movement has a vision for "Every Student Knowing Someone Who Truly Follows Christ."

The Westminster Confession is, "To Know God and to Make Him Known."

The mission statement of my local church is, "We want to glorify God by changing the heart and soul of Northwest Arkansas and the world by producing and releasing spiritual leaders who know and express the authentic Christ."

It is appropriate for others to dream and plan big.

God wants us to dream and plan big. When we keep the boundary of intimacy with God as the purpose of life, He transforms us to be like Him. He transforms our heart to be like His heart. And His heart is for all of humanity. His vision for the world becomes our vision because He is in us, and we are in Him (John 17:22). Our mission may be a tiny role in the world knowing and experiencing Christ. But it is appropriate to dream and plan big because we dream with the heart, soul, and mind of God.

> *"Now to Him who is able to do far more abundantly beyond all that we ask or think, according to the power that works within us."*
>   Ephesians 3:20

> *"Look among the nations! Observe! Be astonished! Wonder!*
> *Because I am doing something in your days—*
> *You would not believe if you were told."* Habakkuk 1:5

Bill Bright had a vision from God of a movement of Christians who would be reaching the world with the gospel. He left his seminary studies and began to recruit students on college campuses to join with him in coming to help change the world through Christ.

Pastor H.D. McCarty tells the story of being in the audience as a student at SMU in the early 1950s when Bill Bright was challenging those attending to come join with him in reaching the world for Christ by joining the staff of Campus Crusade for Christ (Cru). H.D. asked him at the end of the presentation, "What will you use as doctrine?" Bill held up his Bible and said, "We will use this." H.D. laughed at Bill.

Twenty years after that meeting, I was in the audience at University Baptist Church when Pastor McCarty introduced Dr. Bright who was speaking at a week-long series at his church. At that time, Campus Crusade for Christ was on most major university campuses in the U.S. and 65 nations of the world. He recounted the story of laughing at Dr. Bright when he was beginning his ministry. He ended his introduction by saying, "Don't ever laugh at someone who has a vision from God."

God plans and dreams big, and He desires for us to be one with Him in the dreams He has for us.

III. God's Dream for Us in Mission with Him Will Always Prioritize Intimacy with Him Over Intimacy As Mission with Him

God's dream always prioritizes purpose over mission. We have looked at two boundaries that keep relationship with God joyful and pleasurable; the boundary of intimacy with God as the purpose of life and the boundary intimacy as mission with Him. However, we must always recognize and acknowledge that God prioritizes relationship with Him over mission with Him. Oswald Chambers said, "The greatest hindrance to devotion to God is service for Him."

It is absolutely necessary for us to understand this priority.

Both intimacy with God and intimacy as mission with God bring great joy and pleasure. But there is greater joy and pleasure in intimacy with God than there is in intimate mission with Him.

That is the lesson Jesus communicated to his disciples when they returned from their first ministry experience.

> *"Now after this the Lord appointed seventy others, and sent them in pairs ahead of Him to every city and place where He Himself was going to come."*
>
> *"The seventy returned with joy, saying, 'Lord, even the demons are subject to us in Your name.'"*
>
> *"'Nevertheless, do not rejoice in this, that the spirits are subject to you, but rejoice that your names are recorded in heaven.'"*
>
> Luke 10:1, 17, 20

Jesus had prepared the seventy for ministry through their observations of Him and the instructions He had given them. When they returned, their joy at seeing results could hardly be contained. Even the demons were in subjection to them in Christ's name.

But our Lord gave them an admonition that there was a greater joy than the joy they were experiencing in ministry results. The greater joy was that there was an eternal relationship that they experienced with Him. The greater joy was the intimacy of relationship with Him.

I certainly do not want to minimize the joy of intimacy as mission. Intimacy as mission with God has as its result great joy and pleasure. I believe the Lord was also trying to help the disciples to understand that there would be times of ministry in which there would be little or no visible results. There would always be joy in intimacy as mission because of the oneness of togetherness with God. But that joy had no comparison to the joy of the oneness of intimate relationship they experienced with God. That joy was a lasting, eternal joy which could not be taken away.

Mary and Martha were excited that Jesus was coming to their village. Martha was hosting Him in her house. They were probably involved in many of the preparations that we would make in welcoming and making a guest comfortable: cleaning the house, preparing and cooking food, having enough eating utensils, presenting the food, and all the other tasks necessary to serve others well.

*"Now as they were traveling along, He entered a village; and a
woman named Martha welcomed Him into her home. She had a
sister called Mary, who was seated at the Lord's feet, listening to
His word.*

*But Martha was distracted with all her preparations; and she
came up to Him and said, 'Lord, do You not care that my sister
has left me to do all the serving alone? Then tell her to help me.'*

*But the Lord answered and said to her, 'Martha, Martha, you
are worried and bothered about so many things; but only one
thing is necessary, for Mary has chosen the good part, which
shall not be taken away from her.'"*

Luke 10:38-42

Mary had been involved with Martha in the preparations for the serving.
But Mary, in addition to the serving, was doing the necessary, priority
thing, which was good, and could not be taken away. She was seated at the
Lord's feet listening to what He had to share. She was cultivating intimacy
with Him, and that was a higher priority than service for Him.

Martha became distracted by her stewardship for Jesus, and she missed
the most important thing she could be doing – experiencing intimate
relationship with Him.

Martha's testimony could describe the first twenty years of my ministry.

I grew up in a small town in Oklahoma. Attending church was an activity
in which our family was very involved. My father was the Superintendent
of the Sunday School program, and it was our custom to be at church
every Sunday. For me, it was a social gathering. A lot of my friends
attended our church, and it was enjoyable for me to be with them, involved
in the activities of the youth group. But I wasn't involved in the spiritual
focus of our church.

I mentioned earlier that it wasn't until my sophomore year in college that
I came to know Christ personally. College was a time of great spiritual
growth for me. When I graduated, rather than taking a banking position
in Dallas, I decided to join the staff of Campus Crusade for Christ

(Cru). It was, initially, a two-year commitment to help me to focus more intentionally upon my spiritual growth and to learn how to be more effective in helping others to grow spiritually.

I met Beth on my first assignment at the University of Arkansas. We were married several years later.

It seemed that I was on a fast track of opportunities for expanding leadership responsibilities, and I soon found myself at age 28 being the director for the campus ministries in New England, New York, Maryland, Delaware, New Jersey, Virginia, and West Virginia. After serving there for three years, we ministered overseas as the Field Director for nine counties that were known as Eastern Europe.

After seven years, we returned to the United States; and I became the Regional Director for 12 states that comprised the southern and part of the southwestern U.S. We lived in Chapel Hill, NC at that time. I loved what I was doing in ministry and was traveling to campuses in my region almost half of my time.

One day Beth came to me and shared how difficult it was for her when I was gone (and I was gone a lot). Our four children were in elementary school, and Beth shared how much harder it was for her to raise the children in my absence. We talked about this, and I shared that we really needed to pray about my schedule and be open to what God might want us to do. Nothing really changed.

Three months later she came to me, and we had the same conversation again. I shared that I thought that this was a time management issue, so we both got out our schedules and began to look at how I could better organize and schedule my time. I even remember telling her that she had permission to change my plans according to what she felt was best for her and the family. Nothing really changed.

We had the same confusion and conversation again three months later.

About a year and a half from the time of Beth's first conversation with me, a thought struck me one day as I was walking home from a day of ministry on the University of North Carolina campus. "I think she is right." Something was not working. I didn't know exactly what it was, but I needed to give my full attention to dealing with this difficulty and confusion. I began to attentively listen to what Beth was saying, sought counsel from others, and began to seek the Lord as to what needed to change.

It took me a while to realize that I was not living my life according to my priorities.

I could list my priorities in the proper order – God, Beth, our children (Christa, Shane, Kathryn, and Edward), my close male friends, and then the ministry. There was a relational value base that God had given me that was a greater priority than my vocation, which was Christian ministry. But the use of my time did not truly reflect my priorities in life.

I had developed, over a 20-year period, an unhealthy sense of drivenness to prove who I was by what I did. My effectiveness in ministry had become a refuge for me because of my lack of intimacy with God. The bonds of relationship with Beth, our children, and my close friends were suffering also.

I had become like Martha, trying to prove my devotion to Christ by the things I did for Him, rather than the relationship I experienced with Him. I had to learn that the boundary of intimacy with God as the purpose of life was a far higher priority than the boundary of intimacy as mission. Both are important. Both are boundaries that need to be kept for intimacy to be cultivated, but who I am in intimacy with God is of much greater value to Him than what I do for Him (even when the doing is in oneness with Him).

Bobby Vinton had a hit song in 1963 called *Halfway to Paradise*. It was about a boy who was in love with a girl that viewed him simply as a friend. He wanted a deep, loving relationship but she didn't. The chorus to the song included these words, "So near, yet so far away." He was always expectant of the "paradise" of love with her, but it was elusive, and not to be found.

There seems to be a nearness in the priority of mission in oneness with Christ and the priority of intimacy of person with Him. However, they are separate, and there is a gulf between them. In reality, they seem near; and yet they are far away. This does not diminish the importance of service for Christ. Nor does it take away from the desire for results in oneness of mission with Christ. However, service in mission is a distant priority from intimacy of relationship with Christ.

The apostle Paul states this very clearly in Philippians 3:7-8:

> "But whatever things were gain to me, those things I have counted
> as loss for the sake of Christ. More than that, I count all things
> to be loss in view of the surpassing value of knowing Christ Jesus
> my Lord, for whom I have suffered the loss of all things, and
> count them but rubbish so that I may gain Christ."

The surpassing value of knowing and experiencing Christ is the priority of life. Everything else is secondary. The word "rubbish" is translated defecation. Everything else in life is considered as defecation in comparison to the surpassing value of knowing Christ. It is not saying that everything else is defecation. But when something else is compared to the priority of intimacy with God, it will always be a distant second.

Mission is a distant second to intimacy with God.

Our tendency is to say that there should be a balance between intimacy with God and intimacy as mission with God. After all, to say that intimacy with God is always the priority would be to marginalize mission. When we look at the life of Jesus, we see him continually ministering to others. Intimacy as mission with God brings great joy and pleasure.

However, to say that intimacy has to be balanced with mission so that mission will not be marginalized is to marginalize God.

The first commandment says,

> "I am the LORD your God, who brought you out of the land
> of Egypt, out of the house of slavery. You shall have no other
> gods before me. You shall not make for yourself an idol, or any

likeness of what is in heaven above or on the earth beneath or in the water under the earth. You shall not worship them or serve them; for I, the LORD your God, am a jealous God, visiting the iniquity of the fathers on the children, on the third and the fourth generations of those who hate Me, but showing lovingkindness to thousands, to those who love Me and keep My commandments."

Exodus 20:2-6

Anything that becomes a greater priority than intimacy with God is an idol. We are not to worship it or serve it.

No man can serve two masters (Matthew 6:24). Intimacy as mission with God will compete with intimacy with God as the purpose of our life. But mission can only be significant when it is appropriately secondary to intimacy with God.

God's dream for us should always prioritize the purpose of intimacy with Him over intimacy as mission with Him.

But as we examine the boundary intimacy as mission with God there are several things that determine how well we are able to keep that boundary.

The joy and pleasure we experience with God in mission with Him is difficult to communicate to others. I recently spoke at a retreat for a group of seven businessmen who have lunch every Tuesday and have been doing so for 20 years. Every fall, they invite friends of theirs to a retreat at Lake Eufaula in eastern Oklahoma. There were 25 men at the gathering; and, the last morning, we were discussing the joy and pleasure of intimacy as mission. One of the men, Jack, shared a story from his childhood about an afternoon he spent with his father on a tractor.

> "My father loved to farm. He loved his cattle and the cultivating of a crop. When he was in his 80s my dad developed congestive heart failure and was hospitalized. The siblings gathered together to discuss plans for his future care. Could someone return to the farm and care for him there? Could any of us take him into our home? Would there be a nursing home nearby that could provide care for him?

When we asked dad for his input he replied, 'I just want to go back to the farm and be there with my land and my animals.'

We decided that was the best alternative, and we were able to care for him there. He died a week later at home.

It reminded me of a time when I was 12 years old and dad asked me to spend a Saturday afternoon with him on the tractor plowing. My friends were doing exciting things that afternoon, and I really didn't want to spend the afternoon on the tractor. But I grudgingly assented to do so.

When we were on the tractor, I asked dad, 'Why do you enjoy being out here on this tractor plowing the ground?' And he replied, 'Because this is where God is.' And I sarcastically asked him, 'How do you know God is here?' Dad answered, 'I smell Him in the dirt!'"

The joy and pleasure we experience in intimacy as mission with God is very treasured, valued, and cherished. It is a deep relational experience with God that is hard to explain because it is not a formula, a competency to be developed, or knowledge to be gained. It is a relationship of person and mission that we cultivate with God and that He cultivates with us. It can be felt and experienced.

We, too, can sense the hand of God upon what we do. Like Jack's father, who could smell God in the dirt, we can experience unity of mission with God in deep relational, emotional ways.

It is essential in cultivating intimacy with God to keep the boundary of intimacy as mission with Him..

Discussion Questions

1. What prevents you from dreaming God's dream for intimacy as mission with Him?

2. In what ways do you presently sense intimacy as mission with God?

3. In what ways does your life reflect the priority of intimacy with God over unity intimacy as mission with Him?

4. What are the negative consequences of a life where intimacy as mission with God is a priority over intimacy with God?

IV. The Voice of God Through Us

Another aspect of intimacy as mission, that is part of God's design for a destiny with Him, involves His voice spoken by us.

As I mentioned earlier in this book, it was my sophomore year in college when I came to know Christ personally. One of the thoughts that I remember from that meeting in my fraternity house was the words of Jesus when he said, "I came that they might have life, and have it abundantly" (John 10:10b). Those words penetrated my soul. Even though I felt I was living a good life, I knew something was missing. And I knew I could not produce though good behavior, achievements, or good deeds, what was missing. It was as if God spoke to me that evening and said that the abundant life could only be found in Him. His voice was not an audible voice from Him but, nonetheless, the man who spoke those words was a channel through which God clearly communicated His gospel of grace to me.

It was the voice of God, His gospel message, communicated through a follower of Christ, that penetrated my heart that evening.

God's Voice Is the Gospel

In studying the section *Intimacy with God*, we examined the voice that God gives us. There are three criteria of our voice:

- The *deep touch of God* in my life that I have experienced through hearing His greatest "no" for me.

- The *power of God* impressed upon my soul that comes from my deepest weakness.

- The *awesomeness of God* experienced through my poverty of spirit toward Him and others.

God demonstrates Himself to us, not in our greatest victories and achievements, but in our greatest weaknesses, hardships, and sufferings. His power is matured in our weaknesses, not in our greatest accomplishments. The voice He gives us is our story of who He is in our life in a special way. It is like a relational North Star that aligns our priorities and direction.

Our voice isn't directly related to mission. It is about us sharing the foundation of our life, which is intimacy with God.

However, when we examine mission, God gives us His voice.

We have already looked in *Unity As Mission with God* at God's plan for the ages – the redemption of mankind unto Himself.

He loves the world and is desirous that no one would perish (or experience life apart from Him). He has a plan for the ages that is involved in the redemption of mankind unto Himself. When we have unity of mission with God, we will be involved in His plan for mankind. We will have His heart for those who don't know Him. We will be burdened for those who know Him but don't really experience unity with Him. We will desire for the unity of purpose we have with God to be experienced by all of mankind. We will want the whole world to know Him as we do. We will be involved in a mission that is spiritual that transcends our own needs. We will be involved in the unity of fulfillment of good deeds that God directs us in through the unity we have with Him.

In intimacy as mission with God, He gives us a destiny with Him that involves oneness with Him in His plan for mankind.

His voice is the proclamation of that plan through which humanity would come to know and experience Him. That is called the gospel.

> *"For God so loved the world, that He gave His only begotten Son, that whoever believes in Him shall not perish, but have eternal life."* John 3:16

> *"He saved us, not on the basis of deeds we have done in righteousness, but according to His mercy."* Titus 3:5a

> *"But God demonstrates His own love toward us, in that while we were yet sinners, Christ died for us."* Romans 5:8

*"He made Him who knew no sin to be sin on our behalf, so that
we might become the righteousness of God in Him."*
2 Corinthians 5:21

The gospel is the message of God's redemption of us through His grace.
Nothing we could do could ever merit or earn His salvation from our sins.
Acceptance of Christ's death on the cross for our sins is the way we are
able to know and experience God. His desire is that the whole world might
come to know Him.

> *"The Lord is not slow about His promise, as some count
> slowness, but is patient toward you, not wishing for any to perish
> but for all to come to repentance."* 2 Peter 3:9

> *"After these things I looked, and behold, a great multitude which
> no one could count, from every nation and all tribes and people
> and tongues, standing before the throne and before the Lamb,
> clothed in white robes, and palm branches were in their hands;
> and they cry out with a loud voice, saying, 'Salvation to our God
> who sits on the throne, and to the Lamb.'"*
> Revelation 7:9-10

> *"This gospel of the kingdom shall be preached in the whole
> world as a testimony to all the nations, and then the end will
> come."* Matthew 24:14

God's Voice (the Gospel) Is Spoken Through Believers

God's design for the good news of Christ's payment for our sins is that the
message of reconciliation to God through Christ shall be carried to the
whole world through followers of Christ. God has given to us this ministry
of reconciliation of others to know and experience Him.

> *"Therefore if anyone is in Christ, he is a new creature; the old
> things passed away; behold, new things have come. Now all
> these things are from God, who reconciled us to Himself through
> Chris, and gave us the ministry of reconciliation, namely, that*

*God was in Christ reconciling the world to Himself, not counting
their trespasses against them, and He has committed to us the
word of reconciliation.*

*Therefore, we are ambassadors for Christ, as though God were
making an appeal through us; we beg you on behalf of Christ, be
reconciled to God.*

*He made Him who knew no sin to be sin on our behalf, so that
we might become the righteousness of God in Him."*

2 Corinthians 5:17-21

In Christ we are new creatures, reconcilers, and ambassadors.

As a new creature, a new creation, we should no longer live for the values
of the world and the depravity of our flesh. Our desire is to be one with
God as the person He created us to be and with the destiny that we share
with Him in mission. Our focus is no longer centered in self but is a God-
and others-focus.

We are reconcilers who bring others to the truth of right relationship with
God through faith in Christ for the forgiveness of our sin.

Recently, we were having some repairs done on an appliance in our
kitchen. The workman noticed a Christian book, *Ruth*, by Sally Meredith,
on our kitchen counter top. He said, "That looks like an interesting book."
I replied, "Do you know anything about the story of Ruth in the Bible?"
He said that his father was a serious student of the Bible and had shared
many stories from it with him. After about thirty minutes of listening to
him and having the opportunity to share about forgiveness of sin through
Christ, I asked him if he had ever had a time in his life when he felt that he
had placed his faith in Christ for the forgiveness of his sin. He said that he
had done that as a young child.

I asked him, "If you were to die today and go into God's presence, and
God would ask you why do you deserve to be let into heaven, what would
you say to God?" He replied, "I don't deserve to be in heaven. My only
response would be that I believe that Christ died for my sins." I shared that
I believed that he did have a relationship with God because he was trusting

Christ to forgive his sin, and he was not trying to have a relationship with God through good works. It was such a pleasure to affirm to him that he could be confident in his relationship with God because he had been received by God on the basis of his faith in Christ.

What a joy it was to me to be able to share with him about what it is to be made right (reconciled) with God. God desires for us to be His voice of reconciliation to those who don't know him or who are uncertain about their relationship with Christ.

We are also ambassadors of the good news of Christ. An ambassador is a person who is sent to a foreign country to represent the country from which they have come.

I was in Washington, DC recently, and I happened to walk by several embassies. There are ambassadors from other countries who are there to represent their homelands in the United States. Outside of their embassies they prominently display the name of their country and fly their flag. The ambassadors and their staff work tirelessly to reflect the best interest of their homeland to the people and the government of the United States.

Ambassadors are sent from their home country, but they also have authority to speak for their homeland. It is as if the head of their own country were there to make decisions and relate to the people of the country to which they have been sent. The word of the ambassador is the equivalent of the word of the nation they represent. The actions of the ambassador would be considered as those of the heads of the country from which they have come.

A true ambassador is a sent one having authority.

The same is true of us as ambassadors of Christ. He has sent us to the world to reconcile it to Himself. He has given us authority, as His representatives, to share the good news of the gospel of Jesus Christ. We are sent ones with His authority.

He has given His voice to us. It is His voice of reconciling the world unto Himself. In His great plan of the redemption of mankind unto Himself, we are the new creatures in Christ who are reconcilers of the message of

Christ's love and forgiveness to all of mankind. God has appointed us as ambassadors (sent ones) with His authority (representing Him) to proclaim His salvation through Christ throughout the whole world.

We have earlier examined mission as all that we do: vocation, recreation, hobbies, vacation, etc. God had given us a destiny in mission with Him. It is intimacy as mission with Him in all that we do. Within that intimacy as mission, there is also a oneness in His mission of the redemption of mankind unto Himself. God gives us a "slice" of His mission to which we are one with Him as a new creation in Christ, a reconciler, and an ambassador. It is the design of the fullness of life that we have in Christ that His voice of reconciliation to the world is communicated through us as believers in Christ to those who don't know Him.

His voice, the gospel message, that God was in Christ reconciling the world unto Himself, communicated through us as believers in Christ, is His plan for how the world will reached with the good news. Our destiny for what we do in oneness with God will be His voice (of the gospel) communicated through us to mankind as part of the mission He has for us.

Jesus talks about His voice when He discusses the illustration of sheep in John 10.

> *"My sheep hear my voice, and I know them, and they follow me; and I give eternal life to them, and they will never perish; and no one will snatch them out of My hand."* John 10:27-28

His voice is heard by His sheep and they follow Him. He establishes an eternal life relationship.

Earlier, He speaks of the relationship of the shepherd to his sheep.

> *"Truly, truly I say to you, he who does not enter by the door into the fold of the sheep, but climbs up some other way, he is a thief and a robber. But he who enters by the door is a shepherd of the sheep. To him the doorkeeper opens, and the sheep hear his voice, and he calls his own sheep by name and leads them out.*

When he puts forth all his own, he goes ahead of them, and the sheep follow him because they know his voice. A stranger they simply will not follow, but will flee from him, because they do not know the voice of strangers." John 10:1-5

There are strangers that are also called thieves and robbers. They don't enter the doorway to the sheep but climb in some other way. The shepherd enters through the door to the sheep, and they recognize his voice.

Jesus compares His voice to the voice of the thieves and robbers. In John 10:10-11, He makes this comparison again between Himself and thieves and robbers.

"The thief comes only to steal, and kill, and destroy; I came that they may have life, and have it abundantly. I am the good shepherd; the good shepherd lays down His life for the sheep."

God's design for His creation of mankind was an abundant life in Him. Access to relationship with God (and the abundant life that He promised) can only take place because Christ has laid down His life for us. It is through His death on the cross for the forgiveness of our sins that we are able to have eternal life and experience His abundant life.

The voice of Christ speaks of the most difficult, painful, sacrifice He ever had to endure. His voice comes not from His power, authority, and position as God. His voice does not speak to His rights, privileges, and entitlements as the Creator of the universe. His voice comes from His humility, grace, and mercy, as a Servant who has sacrificed His life for the sins of the world.

It is similar to the voice He gives us that is rooted not in power but in weakness, not in self-accomplishment but in service for others. The voice He gives us is not for focus upon the glory of self, but for sacrifice focused toward God and others.

The essence of His voice, His message, is the abundant life that is found only in acceptance of Jesus Christ for the forgiveness of our sins. God's desire is that His voice would go to all nations, to the ends of the earth. It is His plan for the ages, the redemption of mankind unto Himself.

There Is Great Joy and Pleasure in Speaking His Voice

With His voice, God created the universe and the earth and all it contains. God does not grow weary or tired. He doesn't face physical exhaustion because of the enormity of a task. With His voice, He could easily speak the gospel to all the nations. So, why doesn't He simply speak the fulfillment of every nation, tongue, and tribe hearing the good news of Jesus Christ? It is not difficult for Him to do so.

When Jesus was entering Jerusalem prior to His crucifixion, the Pharisees asked Him to rebuke His disciples because they were so enthusiastic and loud.

> *"As soon as He was approaching, near the descent of the Mount of Olives, the whole crowd of the disciples began to praise God joyfully with a loud voice for all the miracles which they had seen, shouting:*
>
> > *'BLESSED IS THE KING WHO COMES IN THE NAME OF THE LORD; Peace in heaven and glory in the highest!'*
>
> *Some of the Pharisees in the crowd said to Him, 'Teacher, rebuke your disciples.'*
>
> *But Jesus answered, 'I tell you, if these become silent, the stones will cry out!'"* Luke 19:37-40

"Blessed is the King who comes in the name of the Lord" in Luke 19:38 is a reference to an Old Testament prophesy from Psalm 118:26. It refers to the coming Messiah. It was a prophesy that was fulfilled by Jesus' triumphant entry into Jerusalem. Jesus was telling the Pharisees this prophesy had to be fulfilled; and, if the group of His disciples were not loudly praising Him, it would have to be done in another way. The rocks would have to cry out with praise.

God could use rocks to communicate His message. His voice of the gospel could be sent to those not knowing Him in ways other than through words of those who believe in Him. Why were people chosen to be communicators of the gospel?

Earlier, we studied the parable of the talents and how the servant who had two talents and the servant that had received five talents both "entered into the joy of the master" (Matthew 25:21, 23). The joy and pleasure of the master was the same for both servants even though the results of their stewardship were differing amounts. There was a joy that the master experienced and shared with his servants in the good stewardship of resources.

The same is true when we have intimacy as mission with God. There is a mutually shared joy and pleasure that we have with God when we are one with Him in what we do. That unity, oneness, and shared destiny with Him bring God great joy and pleasure that is more important to Him than the actual results of what is accomplished. The actual results are incidental to the great joy and pleasure of oneness. God values the relationship of oneness with a good steward who cultivates results superior to the results themselves.

Joy cannot be shared with inanimate objects. A table can't be happy or sad. A computer can break down, but it doesn't become emotionally weary. An apple won't experience pain when you take a bite of it. Emotions are the not the possessions of inanimate objects. Joy is only shared with humanity. That is why God could have designed the stones to cry out praise to Him, but there would be no shared joy and pleasure.

He has chosen us as new creations, reconcilers, and ambassadors as the way through which His voice (the good news) would be communicated to the whole world. It is because of the great joy and pleasure that He experiences with us in the task of His voice going to the world.

Let us never forget the truth that there is always something more important than results. But how could there be something more important than the world being reached with the gospel?

Our relationship with God is more important to Him that anything we could do for Him. Our oneness with Him, in who we are as His creation, is of far greater value to Him than our oneness as mission with Him, a destiny of what we accomplish as one with Him.

Good stewardship of our lives and our resources, in intimacy as mission with God, will involve the sharing of the gospel with others (the voice of God through us). It is the greatest news we have ever received. To accept Christ for the forgiveness of our sins is the greatest decision we will ever make. To help another person experience the life-changing intimacy of relationship with God is the greatest good we could do for them.

The greatest joy and pleasure we could experience in life is the oneness we experience in intimacy with God. There is also oneness we experience in intimacy as mission with God that brings great joy and pleasure to God and to us. God gives us His voice to share with the world. Sharing the gospel is a stewardship that is a special responsibility. It is not a duty or an obligation that we have to perform. The motivation comes from the relational glory that we experience with God as He gives us His heart for those who are apart from Him.

The joy and pleasure that we experience with God when we share the gospel with others is not dependent upon their response. We would greatly desire that all humanity would come to know Christ, but not all people will respond to His voice. A good steward shares Jesus Christ through the power of the Holy Spirit and leaves the results to God.

Faith is a necessary element of good stewardship in sharing the voice of God with others. Our tendency is to think that people might not be interested, that they might be critical of us, that we would be rejected by them, or we might suffer hardship because we shared Christ with them. Those things could happen. But there is also the surety that when we step out in faith to share the good news of the gospel, God is greatly pleased, delighted, and has great joy. We share in His joy and pleasure no matter how people respond to the message.

His voice, shared through us, is the fulfillment of His plan for mankind, that the world would be reconciled unto Himself. It is a mutually shared destiny that we have with Him in which we are privileged to experience intimacy with Him as mission.

Discussion Questions

1. Share opportunities that you have had to communicate the "voice of God" in your vocation.

2. Are there ways, other than your vocation (mission), in which you have been involved in communicating the "voice of God."

3. Is it difficult for you to communicate the "voice of God" to others? If so, what are the reasons?

4. How can you best overcome the barriers you have to communicating the "voice of God" to others?

We are responsible to be good stewards of the gifts, skills, and abilities given to us by God.

I planted, Apollos watered,
but God was causing the growth.

1 Corinthians 3:6

The Boundary of Intimate Stewardship of Resources

I. Intimate Stewardship Resources

There are resources that we are all given: competency, finances, relationships, and time. Resources can used be for our person and for our mission. The responsible use of resources involves an intimacy of stewardship with God. Let's examine these resources.

Competency

Competency refers to gifts, skills, and abilities. It can also refer to aptitudes and proficiencies. It is an aspect of God's unique, special design of our person. It also relates to how our mind thinks about and puts pieces of information and knowledge together. The competencies of an engineer would be quite different from those of a musician. We are responsible to be good stewards of the gifts, skills, and abilities given to us by God. We should pursue their development.

Competency is involved in our personal lives. **It is the personal design resource that God has given to us.** There are competencies related to owning a home: lawn care, cleanliness, mortgage payments, repairs, etc. We want to be a responsible homeowner. There are competencies related to having a car: overall condition, repairs, fueling, payments, etc. We want to responsibly take care of our car. The greatest personal competencies are relational. We want to be responsible to cultivate healthy relationships with others. We desire to be good husbands and wives, parents, children, and be good friends to others.

A major factor in vocational determination is competency. We should pursue vocations in which we have the gifts, skills, and abilities that relate to the work to be performed. There will be a higher correlation of satisfaction in vocations where the majority of what we do is related to our competencies. When our jobs call for us to operate outside of our competencies, then, in the long run, we will have a low level of satisfaction. That would not be a good stewardship of the resource of competency.

Competency has a high correlation to effectiveness. Our desire is to be effective in personal and vocational responsibilities.

The intimate stewardship of the resource of competency means that, in our personal life and in our vocation, we are responsible to grow in and effectively use the competencies that God has given us.

Relationships

Relationship is the priority intimate stewardship resource. It is vitally linked to the heart of God and the Kingdom of Heaven that is His domain.

We can have many types of personal relationships. Don Meredith, author of *Two Becoming One*, speaks of four types of personal relationships: casual, corporate, commitment, and covenant relationships. Let's look at how I have defined these relationships in the book *Forsaking All Others*.

> Most people are involved in relationships that are *casual*. These are informal relationships, not easily measured, where we enter another person's life only briefly and in a surface way. An example is asking a coworker while passing in the hallway, "How are you doing?" and not really looking for more than an "I'm doing fine."

> We are involved in casual relationships many times during a day. There are probably many people that we relate to this way. In fact, we don't even have to have previously known someone to have

this type of casual contact with him or her. Casual relationships can be with many people, but there is not any depth of personal relationship involved.

A *corporate* relationship is expressed in the context of a group in which we are a participant. A group of this nature can be social, relational, or professional. The key to understanding corporate relationships is that the members in the group see the need for the other members. However, there is not necessarily a need for bonding but a need for the complementary skills and talents each person contributes to accomplish a job.

When I was growing up, my parents used to go to a Canasta Club once a month. There were eight couples that played cards together, rotating their meetings from home to home. Each evening began with a potluck dinner; and, when it was at our house, I got to feast with the adults. The meal is all I remember; but for my parents and the other members, it was a social, corporate group. They communicated below a surface level, but there was not a deep relational connecting beyond their club involvement. They appreciated each other's card playing skills and drew upon those skills as they rotated Canasta partners throughout the evening.

Similarly, education today emphasizes the importance of working as a team. My children often received assignments where they were a part of a team that had to accomplish an objective together. It seems, however, that a lot of the time my children ended up doing most of the work while the other team members coasted to a grade in which they put little effort.

A corporate team accomplishing a task is not like the teams my children seemed to encounter in school. There is, on a corporate team, the real sense of the need for the skills of each team member. For the job to be accomplished most effectively, everyone needs each other.

In a *commitment* relationship, we may have daily access to others and cannot accomplish what we want done without them. We do not view these people as any limitation but look to them as a source of help and encouragement. We are committed to each other. We are willing to assume the best of them and to work out the problems/difficulties that arise. The strength of the relationship is found not necessarily in the accomplishment of tasks held in common, but from the like-mindedness of person and purpose. The relationship goes beyond work and is expressed in personal concern.

My friend Gary and I have a commitment-level relationship. Several times a year, we will get away for a day or half-day to just process our relationships with God and being good stewards of mission. He is very involved in a ministry to men. We meet every week to mutually share our life experiences authentically with each other. We are involved in each other's lives and are like-minded in a commitment to be men of godly character. Our relationship is more than being just good friends

We are committed to each other!

The fourth type is a *covenant* relationship. It is characterized by authenticity and trust and accompanied by spoken or written promises. There are four types of covenant relationships:

1. God to His people

2. Husband and wife

3. Parent and child

4. Peers of the same gender

One of the four kinds of potential life-long relationships that we develop is covenant relationship with peers. It is bonds that we make with a dozen or less people. We only have a few of these relationships in our whole lifetime.

Some of the factors we mentioned earlier that make this relationship possible are authenticity, availability, confidentiality, commitment to Christ as one's life, mutual respect for each other, and a focus upon God and others as opposed to self. Peer covenant relationships are sustained by meeting at scheduled times to process what is happening in life both personally and spiritually.

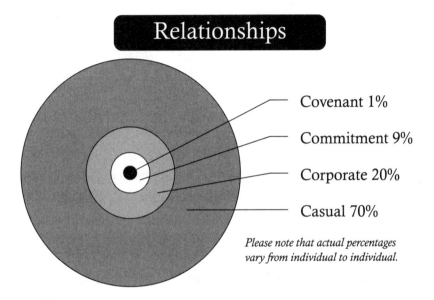

Please note that actual percentages vary from individual to individual.

In talking with others about these four types of relationships, it seems that there are percentages related to the number of people we would have in each category. It has been my experience that the larger the number of relationships the more casual will be the experience with each other. Obviously, casual relationships would be the largest category. As much as 70 percent of the people we encounter are those with whom we will have little or no relationship. Corporate relationships could be as much as 20 percent of the people to whom we relate. The percentage of these relationships can differ due to our work environment (numbers of people), our social contexts, our recreational interests, and other group involvements. Commitment-level relationships will be much fewer because of time, authenticity, and like-minded pursuits. Covenant relationships (1 percent or less) will be fewer than a dozen people in our lifetime (wife / husband, children, and close friendships of the same gender).

In all these personal relationships we experience in life, we want to be an intimate steward of those relationships. Covenant relationships are the priority of our stewardship of relationships. Commitment-level relationships follow as a priority. However, we have to establish a limit to the number of commitment relationships we have. Otherwise, we burn out relationally because the scope of involvement we have in the lives of others exceeds our ability to have quality, healthy relationships. This is particularly true of us in our twenties and thirties.

The key to intimate stewardship of the resource of personal relationship is that we are able to prioritize covenant relationships above commitment relationships, and we are able to limit the number of commitment-level relationships so that we can truly have quality relationships with others.

When we look at relationships vocationally, we also want to be an intimate steward of those relationships. Normally, those relationships fall into the corporate or casual types of relationships. We want to conduct those relationships as a principled people of character, relating to others the way God relates to us. We should be gracious, respectful, honest, compassionate, and helpful. We should also speak the truth in love, hold people accountable, and not be condemning. Gossip and slander should not be a part of our relationships. Forgiveness for wrongs suffered must be a way of life. We cannot dominate, control, and manipulate to get our way by lording over others to get what we want done.

There may be manpower resources assigned to us to accomplish vocational goals. We are to be an intimate steward with God of those people. We can't ask people, over time, to be effective in areas of responsibility of which they do not have competencies. We should be a resource to them (or help provide others as a resource to them) in the accomplishing of their assigned tasks. Demanding that their time commitment be so great that it causes them to violate the boundaries of intimate stewardship of mission is not acceptable.

Oneness in a team is of high value to God. True oneness goes beyond accomplishment of organizational objectives. It is a relational unity that comes from nurturing relationships and treating people the way God relates to us. God will give us those people as coworkers and possibly those we direct. It is incumbent upon us to be intimate stewards with God in the responsibility to relate well to those people.

The keys to intimate stewardship of relationships vocationally is to be a principled person of character, relating to those associated with you casually and corporately as God relates to you, and not lording over those assigned to you but proving to be an example of what it is to serve them and care for them.

I understand that the intimate stewardship of relationships vocationally is not easy and, a lot of the time, can be confusing. Effective results are necessary in order for profitability to ensure employment and expansion. But, when we don't keep the intimate boundary of the stewardship resource of relationships, then the joy and pleasure that comes from the intimacy of oneness with God in what we do becomes sacrificed. Then vocation becomes simply a way to make a living; and comparison, competition, and intimidation become way-of-life behaviors. What was once great joy and pleasure with God becomes work, obligation, and entitlement. God is deeply saddened, and so are we.

Finances

Finance is the appropriate affection resource. It is the resource to which we must always apply appropriate stewardship because it is always competing with intimacy with God as the purpose of life. The world views wealth as the ticket to the train of authority, power, and influence. The world ascribes great value to wealth.

The Kingdom of Heaven ascribes great value to relationships. The keys to relationship are humility, godly character, and serving God and others. Wealth, in the Kingdom of Heaven, is a stewardship entrusted to us. It is a stewardship whether we have great funds or whether our funds are limited. Whether we have an abundance of finances or we have very little, our affection to want more can become an all-consuming obsession.

> *"Do not store up for yourselves treasures on earth, where moth and rust destroy, and where thieves break in and steal. But store up for yourselves treasures in heaven, where neither moth nor rust destroys, and where thieves do not break in or steal; for where your treasure is, there your heart will be also."*

"No one can serve two masters; for either he will hate the one and love the other, or he will be devoted to one and despise the other. You cannot serve God and wealth."

Matthew 6:19-21, 24

Our treasure, what we value most, should be intimacy with God; and we cannot experience intimacy with God unless He is the priority of our life. Wealth, riches, and finances will always be competing with intimacy with God as the priority of our lives. Intimate stewardship of finances is the recognition that all we have is a grace gift from God, and we want to use our finances in such a way that glory is brought to Him.

We all work for finances, which we use for the expenses of our personal lives. We are to be intimate stewards of the finances we earn. We also may be entrusted with finances for what we do vocationally. Companies have budgets from which financial resources are allocated. The parable of the talents is an illustration of the stewardship of financial resources (Matthew 25:14-30).

Here are some other perspectives on finances that have been especially helpful to me.

"…not even when one has an abundance does his life consist of his possessions." Luke 12:15b

"Keep deception and lies far from me, give me neither poverty nor riches; feed me with the food that is my portion, that I not be full and deny You and say, "Who is the Lord?" Or that I not be in want and steal, and profane the name of my God."

Proverbs 30:8-9

We shouldn't spend more than we personally earn. We shouldn't spend more than is entrusted to us vocationally.

It should be our desire to be wise stewards of financial resources. Intimate stewardship of financial resources involves being one with God in the use of the funds that have been provided for us personally and vocationally.

Time

The scarcest and most limited intimate stewardship resource is time. It is only applicable now. We only have today to be an intimate steward of our time. Yesterday is gone. Tomorrow is future. Scripture says that our lifetime is very limited.

> *"As for the days of our life, they contain seventy years, or if due to strength, eighty years, yet their pride is but labor and sorrow; for soon it is gone and we fly away."* Psalm 90:10

> *"Yet you do not know what your life will be like tomorrow. You are just a vapor that appears for a little while and then vanishes away."* James 4:14

It has been my custom (I would like to say daily, but it is frequently) in the mornings to pray and give my time that day to the Lord for whatever He desires. I then develop my to-do list and go for it! However, I am always aware of and sensitive to changes that God has for me. It is more important to me to pursue intimacy with God in the use of my time than accomplishing the things I feel I need to do.

Being an intimate steward of the resource of time involves oneness with God in the daily use of our time. Poor stewardship of our time results when we are not intentional in its daily use.

We lived in England for three years, and the British have a word for having to control the resources of life through self-effort. It is the word "cope." Many times we would ask people how they were doing and the reply would be, "I'm coping." They meant, "I'm managing the resources I have," or, "I'm getting along, not making much progress." Most people live their life simply by "coping."

How different that is than being able to reply, "I have great joy and pleasure in the Lord."

When we have a correct view of God, then we are able to be one with Him in the responsibilities of stewardship that He entrusts to us. Competency, finances, relationships, and time are all valued and processed with God in our personal and missional destiny. There is a stability that we will have in life that can be contrasted by the turmoil and worry of having to control those same resources through self-effort.

For the sake of illustration, I would like to look at each resource as a book that we are to read and understand. The principles from that book should help us in decision-making related to that resource. The more we read and understand about the subject the more effective is our application of it to our life and mission.

The books of Competency, Finances, Relationships and Time are disorganized and laying around on a table. There are several books without titles and they represent other possible resources for which we are responsible in life and mission.

The books need to be picked up and placed in an easily accessible way so that the resources can be best understood and applied. We can place them upright and they can be recognized more easily.

But they can still easily fall over. There is a need for bookends on each side to hold the books firmly in place.

When *Intimate Stewardship of Resources* is examined (Competency, Finances, Relationships, and Time) in the context of *Intimacy With God As the Purpose of Life*, there are two bookends that are necessary in order to be a good steward of resources. The first is *Relating Well to God*, and the second is *Results Are Grace Gifts From God*.

If we desire to be an intimate steward of resources, whether that is personally or vocationally, it is essential to relate well to God and His design for us to always have as the priority of our lives experiencing deep intimacy with Him. It is also essential to understand that when it comes to mission (the accomplishment of intimacy as mission with God), that results are always grace gifts from God.

Discussion Questions

1. Which stewardship resource do you feel is the most important (competency, relationships, finances, and time)? Why?

2. What does it mean to you to be an intimate steward of resources?

3. In what areas of your life do you feel that you are an intimate steward? Why?

II. A Correct View of God Is Essential for Intimate Stewardship of Mission

Let's examine the first bookend that is necessary for intimate stewardship of resources.

Our view of God greatly affects our ability to be an intimate, responsible steward of mission. The great passage of scripture that speaks to intimate stewardship of mission is the parable of the talents.

> *"For it is just like a man about to go on a journey, who called his own slaves and entrusted his possessions to them. To one he gave five talents, to another, two, and to another, one, each according to his own ability; and he went on his journey.*
>
> *Immediately the one who had received the five talents went and traded with them, and gained five more talents. In the same manner the one who had received the two talents gained two more. But he who received the one talent went away, and dug a hole in the ground and hid his master's money.*
>
> *Now after a long time the master of those slaves came and settled accounts with them. The one who had received the five talents came up and brought five more talents, saying, 'Master, you entrusted five talents to me. See, I have gained five more talents.'*

His master said to him, 'Well done, good and faithful slave.
You were faithful with a few things, I will put you in charge of
many things; enter into the joy of your master.' Also the one who
had received the two talents came up and said. "Master, you
entrusted two talents to me. See, I have gained two more talents.'
His master said to him, 'Well done, good and faithful slave. You
were faithful with a few things, I will put you in charge of many
things; enter into the joy of your master.'

And the one also who had received the one talent came up and
said, 'Master, I knew you to be a hard man, reaping where you
did not sow and gathering where you scattered no seed. And I
was afraid, and went away and hid your talent in the ground.
See, you have what is yours.' But his master answered and said
to him, 'You wicked, lazy slave, you knew that I reap where I did
not sow and gather where I scattered no seed. Then you ought to
have put my money in the bank, and on my arrival I would have
received my money back with interest. Therefore take away the
talent from him, and give it to the one who has the ten talents.'

For to everyone who has, more shall be given, and he will have
an abundance; but from the one who does not have, even what
he does have shall be taken away. Throw out the worthless slave
into the outer darkness; in that place there will be weeping and
gnashing of teeth."

Matthew 25:14-30

A talent was a denomination of money. One talent was the equivalent of the annual, average, wage of a person who lived during Christ's lifetime. It was a significant amount of money. The master entrusted his money to his servants. He went on a long journey. It is difficult to know how long he was gone, but it was probably long enough for his investments to reap long-term dividends.

The servant who received one talent hid it in the ground. His justification for doing so was based upon his view of who he perceived the master to be. He knew him to be a hard man, reaping where he did not sow and gathering where he scattered no seed. He told the master he was afraid of him.

The word "hard" refers to touch. It is the condition of skin when it is hard and dried. It is a reference that is used of harshness and roughness. The servant viewed the master as calloused and harsh. "Reaping where you did not sow and gathering where you scattered no seed" are references to a person with an entitlement mentality. It is someone who feels they deserve benefits for which they never worked. His relationship to the master was one of fear.

When we compare the views of the master from the servants with five and two talents, we can assume theirs was the opposite view of the servant with one talent. Rather than viewing the master as calloused and harsh, they viewed him as gentle and humble. Rather than viewing the master as entitled, they viewed the master as gracious. They were not afraid of him but secure in a trusting relationship with him. Let's look further at these contrasts:

VIEW OF GOD

Poor Steward	Good Stewards
Calloused and harsh	Gentle and humble
Entitled	Gracious
Fearful of him	He can be trusted
Isolated from him	Relationship with him
Dominating, manipulating, controlling	Respectful, relational
Against him and made him anxious	For me and I can trust him
Judgmental and condemning	Relational and no condemnation

It is obvious the unfaithful servant did not truly know the character of his master. He said that he knew him, but it was based on false assumptions. It is also clear that he did not have a personal relationship with him. The outer darkness, where there is weeping and gnashing of teeth, is a reference to eternal separation from God.

When God is viewed as harsh, calloused, entitled, and not to be trusted, then there is not good, faithful stewardship of mission. When God is perceived as domineering, controlling and manipulating in order to get his way, relationship will be based upon performance, works, obligation, and entitlement. The unfaithful servant was a poor steward because his view of

God was one of a worldly master who uses authority to lord over those for whom he has responsibility. He viewed his master as willful, always trying to get his way. He could not accept the true character of his master as gentle, humble, and a servant to him. Grace and relationship were foreign to him because he could only understand works and performance.

The mission (the master's money entrusted to a servant) is joyous when there is oneness with each other in the doing of it. God doesn't want us to perform for Him. He is not trying to fix us to become perfect. He is not dominating us to get what He wants. His greatest desire is that we could experience His person as the purpose of our life and experience oneness together in mission. His destiny for us, and our desire to be one with Him in that, is of great joy and pleasure to God. He values relationship and stewardship to be experienced in oneness with Him. Otherwise, relationship and stewardship with God will become duty and obligation.

In the Greek language, he words grace (*charis*) and joy (*chara*) come from the same root word *char*. They are very closely related in relationship with each other. In the parable of the talents, the poor steward viewed the master as entitled. He "reaped where he had not sown and gathered where he scattered no seed." This attitude could also be expressed as willful. A willful master would be one who always had to get his way. Performance was what was important and relationship would always be secondary. The poor steward, viewing the master as willful, would assume him to be harsh and demanding. After all, he thought, results were what the master really cared about.

However, the joy of the master is shared with the good stewards. It was the intention of the resources they were given to be one with the master in their stewardship. Relationship with him was a grace gift to them, and the result of their stewardship was sharing the joy that the master had with them as they related well to him.

In vocation, it is important to know our boss and his or her desires. It will affect the outcomes for which we labor.

We can't be good stewards in life (purpose and mission) if we don't know the Master (God) well and His desires for us.

Discussion Questions

1. What are truths about God that motivate you to be a good steward?

2. Describe a time in your life when you experienced the joy and pleasure of intimate stewardship of resources in mission with God.

III. Results Are Grace Gifts from God

In order to fully experience intimate stewardship of resources, it is necessary to understand that results are God's responsibility, not ours. *Results Are Grace Gifts From God* is the other bookend that allows us to be intimate stewards of resources.

There is a wonderful passage in the Bible that communicates that results are God's responsibility.

> *"For when one says, 'I am of Paul,' and another, 'I am of Apollos,' are you not mere men? What then is Apollos? And what is Paul? Servants through whom you believed, even as the Lord gave opportunity to each one.*
>
> *I planted, Apollos watered, but God was causing the growth. Now he who plants and he who waters are one; but each will receive his own reward according to his own labor.*
>
> *For we are God's fellow workers; you are God's field, God's building."*
>
> 1 Corinthians 3:4-6, 8, 9

The context of this passage refers to personal spiritual growth through the ministry of others who help us. The illustration is of a plant that needs to be nourished and cultivated. Many people can be involved in helping a plant to grow. If a seed, through cultivation, becomes a healthy, mature plant, it is a gift from God. The end result of spiritual labor in the lives of others is in God's hands, not ours.

Why do some plants grow and others die, even when the same labor is involved with each? It is because spiritual growth cannot be viewed as an entitlement. Performance plus hard work, in the spiritual Kingdom of Heaven, does not guarantee growth and maturity. Growth and maturity are grace gifts from God.

I grew up in small town in Oklahoma that was partially a rural farming community. There were a lot of wheat fields surrounding me. You could ask any farmer, "Will your hard work be a guarantee of a good crop?" And the answer would always be, "No." A seasoned, experienced farmer is knowledgeable of what he has to do in order to cultivate a crop. He understands the crop itself and all the uniqueness involved in its growth. At the proper time, he tills the soil. He plants the seed at the correct depth. The field is watered and nourished appropriately. He protects the crop from predators. Weeds are removed. Then, there is a specific, short period of time in which the crop can be harvested.

The farmer can do all the right things and lightening strike the crop, it burn up, and be completely destroyed just before the harvest time. Hail can do the same destruction. Drought can be equally devastating.

Every farmer knows that when a crop is harvested there are elements beyond his control that allow the plants to become mature and be harvested. He cannot live with a high sense of entitlement that his efforts have to have the desired results he wants, because results are grace gifts from God.

The second illustration of results as grace gifts is in the passage following the one we just examined.

> *"According to the grace of God which was given to me, like a wise master builder I laid a foundation, and another is building on it. But each man must be careful how he builds on it. For no man can lay a foundation other than the one which is laid, which is Jesus Christ.*

Now if any man builds on the foundation with gold, silver,
precious stones, wood, hay, straw, each man's work will become
evident; for the day will show it because it is to be revealed with
fire, and the fire itself will test the quality of each man's work.

If any man's work which he has built on it remains, he will
receive a reward. If any man's work is burned up, he will suffer
loss; but he himself will be saved, yet so as through fire."

1 Corinthians 3:10-15

This passage is in the context of missional (vocational) intimate
stewardship of resources. It is a homebuilder beginning the construction
and deciding upon the materials to use. Gold, silver, and precious stones
are quality construction materials. Wood, hay, and straw are inadequate
material for construction. There will be a testing of the house as to quality
of its construction.

Tornados, hurricanes, floods, fires, earthquakes, etc. can easily destroy
quality-constructed homes. Even master homebuilders can be wise in the
use of quality materials, and something happens that is out of their control
that will cause damage to the house.

A covenant friend of mine is a wise, master builder. He specializes in home
renewal. He shared with me about a man who hired him to do some major
renovations and an addition to his house. The planning stage and the
construction went really well. My friend spent extra time and even hired a
worker to be there full-time at the house to ensure that quality construction
was being done according to the owner's desires.

Upon the completion of the construction, the owner did not pay. In fact,
he refused to even discuss payment. My friend had sub-contractors that
needed to be paid as well as his own expenses. The lack of payment went
on for months. Many people suffered because of the lack of funds that
were contracted to be paid. This was not the outcome my friend expected
for a job that he felt was well done.

Eventually, a sub-contractor threatened the homeowner with a lawsuit and
he decided to pay. When the result of a job well-done is payment on time it
is a grace gift from God.

If results are grace gifts from God, then do I have any responsibility for results? Why should I labor in intimate stewardship of resources when results are always God's responsibility?

There is a correlation between results (which are always grace gifts from God) and our labor in the intimate stewardship of resources. Our responsibility is to cultivate results but realize that we do not have an entitlement to them. There is no guarantee that our stewardship will produce the results that we desire.

The farmer cultivates results by doing the best job he can in knowing the plant: the seasons to plant and harvest, the irrigating, the protection of the crop, maintenance of equipment, etc. He does this not just through self-effort but also in intimate stewardship with God. The farmer is a good intimate steward of results. However, he has no guarantee that his intimate stewardship of results will produce the outcome he desires. Results are grace gifts from God.

The builder, likewise, can have the best plans, materials, well-skilled laborers, etc., to construct the house. He can have an intimate stewardship of resources with God, but he is not guaranteed the outcome he would desire. A well-constructed home, pleasing to the owner (and paid for) is a grace gift from God.

Eating healthy foods and exercising regularly should contribute to a longer, healthier life. We should cultivate a longer, healthier life through proper exercise and diet. But the reality is that every day we have is a grace gift from God.

Let me say it again: Our responsibility for results, in intimate stewardship of resources, whether personally or vocationally, is to cultivate results. Results are not entitlements. Results are grace gifts from God.

To be good stewards that cultivate results, it is essential to understand that the resources we have been given are not to be used to get what we want out of life. Life is not about an unhealthy drivenness in which we accomplish more than everyone else. If so, then we will have placed a bookend of "self-accomplishment" around the resources given to us and squandered the opportunity to experience that life, which, in its essence, is relational.

The world will always be about performance and accomplishment. It will be a selfish focus upon "me." If we get caught up in this vicious work ethic, then there will be no intimacy with God and others. At the end of our lives, there will be emotional instability where we find ourselves saying, "Is this all there is to life? There has to be something more." We will feel a deep regret that haunts us because we invested in self rather than God and others. No amount of accomplishment will have been able to compensate for relational intimacy with God and others.

There will also be the possibility that mission becomes the means to identity, recognition, fame, and fortune. The bookend of *Results Are Grace Gifts From God* will have been replaced with the bookend of *Look Out For Number One* – out think, out work, out perform everyone else. There is no intimacy as mission with God because you will have determined the outcomes and they drive how resources are applied. There is no sense of joy and pleasure in what you are experiencing together with God as you labor with Him in His desires. The bar of accomplishment will always be raised, and it becomes too easy to use control, manipulation, and domination of others as means to further excel. The older we get, the more entitled we become. After all, we should have received more, been recognized more, and been appreciated more. "More" defines mission when there is no unity with God. Results will have been the priority over relationships. We will have wanted "more," but we will have become people defining ourselves by how little we feel we did receive. There will be no gratefulness or humility but anger, bitterness, and condemnation of others.

When results are grace gifts from God, then we can be good stewards that cultivate results and trust God to lead, guide, direct, and provide. Intimacy with God is always more important than results. Intimacy in mission with God is always more important than results. Experiencing joy and pleasure relationally in Him is His eternal design for His creation of us.

The surpassing value of knowing and experiencing Christ is of far greater value than any accomplishment we could ever perform!

Discussion Questions

1. Why can't we equate hard work with guaranteed results? Give an illustration from your own life.

2. What does it mean to cultivate results as an intimate steward of resources but not have an entitlement that good results must take place?

3. What are the greater things we miss when our life is lived through works, performance, obligation, and entitlement?

4. What grace gift results from God have you experienced in your life and mission?

IV. Painful Results
Are Grace Gifts from God

How can results that are painful, saddening, and hurtful be grace gifts from God? Can suffering, grieving, and mourning be results that are gifts from God?

It is easy to recognize a grace gift when it is something desirable. How exciting it is when one has a deep desire and has prayed and waited many years to be married, and God brings that person to them. When an operation is successful and the pain of many years is relieved, how gracious we recognize God to be. If a child is strong-willed, defiant, and errant in their ways, how encouraging it is when they turn from those ways and choose God over self and relationship over rebellion.

But what of the outcomes that are not desired: the marriage that never takes place, the operation that is not successful, and the child that remains astray? What about the illness for which there is no cure, the untimely death of a child, or the lifetime of rejection from the relative or friend with whom we so desperately seek affirmation?

When results seem negative, is that a punishment from God upon us? If the outcomes are not what we had anticipated, is there something wrong with us? Do we lack faith?

Should we turn from God when we don't get our way? Why should God allow evil and suffering to happen to us when we love Him and have surrendered our lives to Him?

Does grace only work in the good times? Or does God's grace apply to all of life? Are the difficult times, the suffering, times of loss, and sadness, times when grace is sufficient? Are all results in God's hands?

How can there be joy in the midst of sadness, loss, and grief?

I know God is sovereign. He is all-knowing, loving, and kind. He is gentle and humble. But, emotionally, it is hard to reconcile the truth of His person and His actions toward me as good when I encounter hardship and sadness.

Grace is so good. It is so wonderful because there is no performance attached to it. Perfection is not a criterion for it. In fact, the realization of imperfection and unworthiness actually awakens the realization for and acceptance of grace.

The goodness of grace is not difficult to recognize when things go well because we have the assumption that, if we are good, life will go well. The goodness of grace is difficult to recognize when things go badly because we question why sadness, suffering, and pain should come to us from God who is good.

God is always good no matter what the circumstances. There is no entitlement to a carefree, happy, life of comfort. The purpose of life is joyful, intimate relationship with God, not the elimination of difficulties that will bring pleasant circumstances. Jesus said,

> *"These things I have spoken to you, so that in Me you may have peace. In the world you have tribulation, but take courage; I have overcome the world."* John 16:33

In this context, the word "tribulation" means grievous affliction or distress, a pressure of burden upon the spirit.

Psychiatrist Elisabeth Kubler-Ross, in her book, *On Death and Dying*, introduced five stages of grief that most people experience:

Denial – "This can't be happening to me."

Anger – "Why is this happening? Who is to blame?"

Bargaining – "Make this not happen, and in return I will _____."

Depression – "I am too sad to do anything."

Acceptance – "I'm at peace with what happened."

Everyone does not grieve in the same way, and we don't necessarily have to go through each stage in order to heal. Kubler-Ross also says, "There is not a typical response to loss because there is no typical loss. Our grieving is as individual as our lives."

God nurtures us in different ways, through different circumstances, over time, to experience His sufficient grace.

Job understood that there was something of greater importance and value than the comforts, pleasures, and the abundance the world had to offer.

> *"'Naked I came from my mother's womb, naked I'll return to the womb of the earth. God gives, God takes. God's name be ever blessed.' Not once through all this did Job sin; not once did he blame God."* Job 1:21-22, The Message

> *"Though He slay me, yet will I trust in Him."*
> Job 13:15a, King James Version

It is as if there is a two-cylinder engine inside us that is continually firing. One cylinder fires and says, "The Lord gives." The second cylinder fires and says, "The Lord takes away." As we move through life, the motor is continuously firing: the Lord gives, the Lord takes away, the Lord gives, the Lord takes away, the Lord gives, the Lord takes away. And our response, whether He gives or whether He takes away, is, "Blessed be the name of the Lord!"

Intimacy with God is pleasures and sorrows shared.

When we go our own way apart from God, there are consequences that God will not remove. Even though we will at times say "No" to God, He still respects our person. We are still created in His image, according to His likeness (Genesis 1:26). God is not angry with us nor does He punish us. He does not condemn us or shame us. He is always good, kind, gentle, and humble toward us. He is always gracious with us. All of life with God is grace gifting from Him. It has nothing to do with performance for Him.

Sadness is an appropriate response to unmet expectations. It was on many occasions the response of our Lord.

> *"Therefore, when Mary came where Jesus was, she saw Him, and fell at His feet, saying to Him, 'Lord, if You had been here, my brother would not have died.' When Jesus therefore saw her weeping, and the Jews who came with her also weeping, He was*

deeply moved in spirit, and was troubled, and said, 'Where have you laid him?' They said to Him, 'Lord come and see.' Jesus wept." John 11:32-35

"And He took with Him Peter and James and John, and began to be very distressed and troubled. And He said to them, 'My soul is deeply grieved to the point of death; remain here and keep watch.' And He went a little beyond them, and fell to the ground and began to pray that if it were possible, the hour might pass Him by. And He was saying, 'Abba! Father! All things are possible for You; remove this cup from Me; yet not what I will, but what You will.'" Mark 14:33-36

When tragedy strikes, we wish that it would not have happened. What could have been done differently? But Jesus experienced tragedy, and it was the will of His Father. Sadness, distress, and mourning are the companions of suffering. Life can be an agony that has been set before us. But whatever God has for us, agony or ecstasy, there is joy and pleasure in the intimate bonding we experience in Him.

When sadness occurs in my life, there is a setting that I go to in my mind. It is a beautiful beach at sunrise. It is still dark as I am there just before dawn, but more and more light is being revealed as the sun begins to rise. There is the soothing sound of the waves breaking upon the shore. The shore is warm, and the ocean breeze is cool.

However, I feel isolated and alone. There is no one else there. I am emotionally troubled. I am discouraged and depressed.

As I walk out into the ocean, I am overwhelmed with the sadness and mourning of the disappointments and circumstances of people. Failure seems all around me, and I am taking it personally. I am fearful because I have awareness that I cannot control that which I deeply care about. I stop when the water is at my shoulders, and I see a wave that it is about to come over me.

It is an **emotional wave of rest** that comes over me and surrounds my heart. Its substance is God's grace, and it floods my emotions. It can be experienced because of the ongoing, full surrender of my heart to God. It is a feeling of stability when circumstances are in chaos around me. It is a restfulness of my heart that I cannot explain. I believe that there are three special ways that God, through His grace, relationally works within my heart when I encounter deep pain and suffering.

The **first aspect** of the emotional wave of rest is **God's love being poured out within my heart**. God loves me for who I am and not for what I do for Him. His desire is that I would love Him for who He is and not for what He does for me. God's love is not earned through my good works. It is a grace gift that I choose to receive that is not attached to my performance.

God's love is the greatest affirming attribute of His person. It is far more motivating than works, entitlement, or obligation. On my behalf, as His creation, God bears, believes, hopes, and endures all things. His love for me is unfailing. There is never anything that I could do that would take away the love God has for me.

When times are rough, and, emotionally, we don't think we can continue on, God demonstrates His love for us.

> *"And not only this, but we also exult in our tribulations, knowing that tribulation brings about perseverance; and perseverance, proven character; and proven character, hope; and hope does not disappoint, because the love of God has been poured out within our hearts through the Holy Spirit who was given to us."* Romans 5:3-5

One summer I was making a ministry change that required that our family move from Chapel Hill, NC to northwest Arkansas. Our house in North Carolina sold in May to a friend of ours from our church. The closing date was the end of the first week in July, and we would then move in to a house in Arkansas that had accepted our bid.

The latter part of May through the first week in July, I was directing a leadership training center for college students from all over the United States that was held in Branson, Missouri. As soon as our children could be released from school for the summer, I returned back from Branson to help pack and drive us as a family to Branson.

We had an incredible summer of ministry! But our family was physically tired at the end.

The final morning of the leadership training center, I went down to the office we had in a large, old hotel where we were housed. As I was reflecting in a devotional time, a fax came over our machine. We rarely received faxes, so I looked at it and saw that it was from the person who bought our house. It was the closing date, and he had decided to back out from purchasing our house. I called him to find out what was happening; and, as I talked with him, I learned that he just did not feel comfortable about purchasing our house.

I was devastated!

It was as if an emotional shock wave had hit me. What do we do next? How do we sell our house when we no longer live there? Do we still move? What about the house we have purchased in Arkansas? Where do we go next?

As I shared with Beth and the children, it was a difficult time for them also. There was so much uncertainty, and we seemed directionless.

That morning as I walked in to direct our last staff meeting of the summer, emotionally I was at rock bottom. I began to honestly share with the staff what had just taken place. I couldn't make sense of it. I had no idea what to do next, was emotionally drained from this circumstance, and physically drained from a summer of intense ministry.

I also shared with the staff that I knew that God was always good. His goodness was always extended toward us; and He could take any circumstance, even this tragic one, and use it for His good. I also shared that I knew God loved me. His love is everlasting and unfailing. Nothing could separate me from God's love and the eternal bond we share together.

At one of the most difficult, worrisome times in my life, I had an inner peace because I was experiencing the love that God had for me. It was as if, in my innermost being, God was personally caring for and demonstrating His love for me. That is how He relates to us with His all-sufficient grace.

The second is joy inexpressible that comes from my heart in the midst of sadness. It is not the confident joy of expectation fulfilled but the sorrowful joy of suffering shared with Christ. He had a joy, set before Him, that enabled Him to suffer on the cross (Hebrews 12:2). As I reflect upon Him and the hostility of men toward Him I can appropriate that joy of intimacy with Him in His sufferings. Paul said it this way,

> *"That I may know Him and the power of His resurrection and the fellowship of His sufferings, being conformed to His death."*
> Philippians 3:10

There is a fellowship with Christ in suffering that we cannot fully understand, and there is a joy in suffering that we can intimately experience in Christ. It is not the "hallelujah" type of joy. It is the steadfast, immoveable, endurance kind of joy that settles my heart. I weep. I am very sad. I don't know if I will get over the grief or suffering; but it is okay because I am in Him, and He is in me. He cares, and He is sad; and we will make it through this. He gives me a joy that is very real.

Peter describes it as a joy inexpressible and full of glory.

> *"And though you have not seen Him, you love Him, and though you do not see Him now, but believe in Him, you greatly rejoice with joy inexpressible and full of glory."* 1 Peter 1:8

James referred to it as a joy that can be experienced in the midst of difficulties.

> *"Consider it all joy, my brethren, when you encounter various trials."* James 1:2

We can have joy in the midst of sadness and trials. It is a joy that Christ experiences. We can share with Him together in our suffering and experience His joy which is inexpressible.

The **third aspect** of the emotional wave of rest is **a peace that passes all understanding**. God in His grace takes my troubled heart and gives me peace. How can I have peace in my heart when an emotional and spiritual war rages around and within me? I am bothered and worried because I cannot control that which I deeply care about. My emotions are in conflict with what I know to be true. They seem to overwhelm me.

However God is greater than my troubled heart; and His grace is sufficient for whatever I am facing. Paul wrote to the Philippians,

> *"And the peace of God, which surpasses all comprehension, will guard your hearts and your minds in Christ Jesus."*
>
> Philippians 4:7

Peace for the troubled heart is also mentioned in John 14:27.

> *"Peace I leave with you; My peace I give to you; not as the world gives do I give to you. Do not let your heart be troubled, nor let it be fearful."*

The emotional wave of rest now washes over my saddened heart. God pours out within my heart His love through the Holy Spirit, He gives me His joy which is inexpressible, and I have a peace within which passes all understanding.

There are times when we know that God is all that we need, and it is usually when He is all that we have. His grace is sufficient when He is all that we have and need.

Blessed be the name of the Lord!

There is a **second wave of grace** that is now is coming toward me. It is the wave of **affirmation of godly character**. It will soon be washing over my soul.

This wave is one of confidence within my person that the sadness I feel, that I give back to Christ, is resulting in godly character within me. Tribulation is producing perseverance, and perseverance is developing proven character. Proven character results in a hope that God will be glorified (Romans 5:3-4).

In my tribulation, I am becoming like Him. My image is becoming conformed to His image. The purpose of my creation to experience intimacy with God is being experienced in my soul in the midst of my tribulation. My identity is in Him and not my circumstances. I am affirmed that His attributes are being reflected in my person and godly character is the result.

The hymn, *It Is Well with My Soul*, was written by a Chicago lawyer, Horatio G. Spafford. It was written during the most difficult period of Spafford's life. His only son died in 1870 at the age of four because of scarlet fever. A year later, his business collapsed because of the Great Chicago Fire.

Aware of the toll that these disasters had taken on the family, Horatio decided to take his wife and four daughters on a holiday to England. Not only did they need the rest, D. L. Moody, the famous evangelist and also their close friend, needed their help with a campaign he was to have in London. They planned to join Moody in late 1873. So, the Spaffords traveled to New York in November from where they were to catch the French steamer *Ville du Havre* across the Atlantic. Just before they set sail, a last-minute business development forced Horatio to delay. Not wanting to ruin the family holiday, Spafford persuaded his family to go on as planned. He would follow later.

Before his wife, Anna, and their four children reached England, the ship collided with another ship. The ship sank in only 12 minutes, and 226 lives were lost. Spafford received a telegram from his wife in Wales. It read, "Saved alone."

Upon hearing the terrible news, Horatio Spafford boarded the next ship out of New York to join his bereaved wife. During his voyage, the captain of the ship called him to the bridge. "A careful reckoning has been made," he said, "and I believe we are now passing the place where the *du Havre* went down. The water is three miles deep."

Horatio then returned to his cabin and wrote the lyrics of his great hymn:

> When peace, like a river, attendeth my way,
> When sorrows like sea billows roll;
> Whatever my lot, Thou hast taught me to say,
> It is well, it is well with my soul.
>
> Though Satan should buffet, though trials should come,
> Let this blest assurance control,

That Christ hath regarded my helpless estate,
And hath shed His own blood for my soul.

My sin, oh the bliss of this glorious thought!
My sin, not in part but the whole,
Is nailed to His cross, and I bear it no more,
Praise the Lord, praise the Lord, O my soul!

For me, be it Christ, be it Christ hence to live:
If Jordan above me shall roll,
No pang shall be mine, for in death as in life
Thou wilt whisper Thy peace to my soul.

And Lord haste the day, when my faith shall be sight,
The clouds be rolled back as a scroll;
The trump shall resound, and the Lord shall descend,
Even so, it is well with my soul.

Chorus:

It is well with my soul
It is well, it is well with my soul.

There can be peace in our soul whatever calamity faces us. It is a peace
that can only come from God. We cannot humanly produce that which
is an attribute of God. When our soul is bonded to the soul of God, then
our identity is in who He says we are: deeply loved, completely accepted,
totally forgiven, God is for us – not against us. It is then that the ship of the
value or worth of our person can be anchored to the truth of who we are in
Christ.

There can be peace in our soul, and the realization that God is conforming
us to His image. We are becoming like Him through godly character.

The **third wave** that goes over me in the midst of my pain and suffering is
the wave of competency at what matters most in life. It is a wave related
to my mind that gives a sense of direction to my life, but the direction
is not linear with the next best steps that should be taken. It is a much
deeper emotion and satisfaction about what I should do next. The sense of

competency about what to do relates more to a relationship that to a focus upon things to accomplish. It is an abiding in Christ who always relates in grace. That abiding in Him, oneness with Him, and intimacy with Him is the purpose of our creation by Him.

God's greatest pleasure for us is intimacy with us. His desire is that our greatest pleasure would be intimacy with Him. There is no greater competency that we could experience in life than intimacy with God.

There is competence in stewardship that is necessary for the cultivation of results. Competence in mission with Christ is very important. But there is something more important than results in mission. It is intimacy with Christ. It is abiding in Him.

Earlier, we examined the priority of intimacy with Christ over service in mission with Him in the story of Mary and Martha.

> *"Now as they were traveling along, He entered a village; and a woman named Martha welcomed Him into her home. She had a sister called Mary, who was seated at the Lord's feet, listening to His word.*
>
> *But Martha was distracted with all her preparations; and she came up to Him and said, 'Lord, do you not care that my sister has left me to do all the serving alone? Then tell her to help me.'*
>
> *But the Lord answered and said to her, 'Martha, Martha, you are worried and bothered about so many things; but only one thing is necessary, for Mary has chosen the good part, which shall not be taken away from her.'"*

Luke 10:38-42

Martha had become obsessed with the details of serving our Lord. The competency of her ministry to and for Christ prevented her from experiencing intimacy with Him. Jesus told her that there was "only one" necessary thing; the good part, which could not be taken away from her. It was the priority of intimate relationship with Him. Mary, her sister, was experiencing this intimate relationship.

The greatest, most important, competency is intimacy with God.

There is a distance in the priority of intimacy with Christ and the stewardship of resources in Him. We constantly have to be on guard in trying to be competent in effectiveness of mission and it not becoming a greater priority than intimacy with Christ.

If effectiveness becomes the goal of our life, then performance for Christ can easily replace intimate relationship with Him.

When we cannot control life and it seems to be crumbling around us, we are brought to the realization that there is something more important in life than personal or mission results. It is a competency that is irreplaceable, priceless, that cannot be accomplished by our best efforts. It is the grace gift of intimacy with Christ that is not circumstantial, programmed, nor in the future. It is the grace gift of relationship that is sufficient for us in the midst of the difficulty.

God gives us the awareness of His presence and His sufficiency in our lives. It is an awareness of the most important competency in life – intimacy with Him. He is affirming, comforting, and in Him we have rest.

As I allow the waves of emotional rest, godly character, and competency at what is most important in life to wash over me; I look toward the shore, and there is Christ with outstretched arms awaiting me. I choose to come to Him and experience Him. There is the bond of relationship with God that is grace that is sufficient.

> *"And He has said to me, 'My grace is sufficient for you,*
> *for power is perfected in weakness.'"* 2 Corinthians 12:9a

My heart can be at rest no matter how troubled the world is around me. We walk away together, as one, Him in me, I in Him, to face whatever challenges to our relationship that the present and future hold. As a result of our abiding, I am able to share with others how wonderful Christ is and the love and forgiveness that is only found in Him.

Grace is abundant and grace is sufficient. We experience God's love when His grace is abundant and sufficient, but our love for God is experienced by Him when we abide in Him as we experience His grace that is sufficient.

Discussion Questions

1. How can you have joy in the midst of suffering and trials?

2. Share the most difficult time in your life when you found God's grace to be sufficient.

3. Why is intimacy with God the greatest competency in life? How does that make sense in the midst of tragedy and loss?

V. Phenomenon
Is a Grace Gift from God

There are times when God works in very evident, out-of-the-ordinary ways. His results are always grace gifts, but sometimes the magnitude of them to us can be surprising and sometimes overwhelming. I call that phenomenon.

Biblical examples of phenomenon are God parting the Red Sea in Exodus 14:21-22, Jesus feeding the 5,000 in John 6:1-14, the man blind from birth receiving his sight in John 9:6-7, and Jesus halting a storm in Mark 4:35-41. Scriptures are filled with spiritual and personal phenomenon. Let's look at one of my favorites.

> *"Simon Peter said to them, 'I am going fishing.' They said to Him, 'We will also come with you.' They went out and got into the boat; and that night they caught nothing. But when the day was now breaking, Jesus stood on the beach; yet the disciples did not know that it was Jesus.*
>
> *So Jesus said to them, "Children, you do not have any fish, do you?" They answered Him, 'No.' And He said to them, 'Cast the net on the right-hand side of the boat, and you will find a catch.' So they cast, and then they were not able to haul it in because of the great number of fish."*
>
> John 21:3-6

Simon Peter had been a professional fisherman before he became a disciple of Christ. He had fished all night, using all the skill and resources available to him and had no fish. Jesus directed him to cast his net in a specific location and he pulled in almost more fish than the net could hold. Verse 11 says that Simon Peter counted the fish, and there were 153 large fish. Why would he count the fish? I am an avid fisherman, and I think I know the reason.

When I go fishing with my friends, most of the time we count the number of fish we catch. The larger ones we measure their length and weigh them.

We all know the largest fish we have caught and the largest number we have caught in a single outing.

It was because this was the largest catch Simon Peter had ever caught.

It was a phenomenon!

Phenomenon happens in our lives and mission. It may not happen on a grand scale to us. There can be times where it is simple things that God does. Normally, we experience phenomenon as extraordinary and surprising.

Phenomenon Should Be Desired but Not Sought After

We should dream and plan big. Our desire should be for God to do mighty things in our lives and in our mission of oneness in Him and with Him. We should be intimate stewards of the resources that God has given us. We should cultivate or nurture results. However we should be very cautious that we do not develop an entitlement to the results for which we have dreamed and planned and cultivated. Results are in God's hands. They are grace gifts from Him. Where is the relationship with faith and results? If we have enough faith, won't we see the results we dream of and for which we labor? After all, faith can move mountains.

> *"And He said to them, "'Because of the littleness of your faith;*
> *for truly I say to you, if you have faith the size of a mustard*
> *seed, you will say to this mountain, "Move from here to there,"*
> *and it will move; and nothing will be impossible to you.'"*
> Matthew 17:20

Is it our faith that causes results? Does our lack of faith results in unmet expectations?

Faith always needs an object. When the object of our faith is God, nothing is impossible because God is the author and creator of all things. He holds the universe in His hands. He can move mountains simply by commanding them to move. Do I have faith in God that He can do that? Yes. Does that mean that He will choose to do that if I pray in faith believing? Not necessarily so. He will do what He sovereignly chooses to do for His glory. The key is that I am praying and believing in faith according to His will.

> *"Whatever you ask in my name, that will I do, so that the father may be glorified in the Son. If you ask me anything in My name, I will do it."* John 14:13-14

Sometimes God's answers to my prayers are "No." Many times His answers to my prayers are "Wait." He grants my requests when it is according to His will, and the answer always brings glory to Him.

Phenomenon is not as a result of our faith – even though it could happen when our faith is in God and it is according to His will. Phenomenon is and always will be a grace gift from God.

There is the tendency to think that phenomenon is the authenticator of God's will and His blessing. Favorable results can be viewed as the proof of intimate relationship with God. If we aren't seeing anticipated results, then there is something wrong with us spiritually. This is particularly true when we know others who are experiencing far greater results than us. However, phenomenon is not the proof of intimate relationship with God.

Every two years, all of the U.S. national staff of Cru gather together for our Staff Conference. One of the highlights of our time together is the sharing of our worldwide ministries. It is a tremendously encouraging and visionary time as our staff share what God is doing throughout the world. However, it can also become a time of contrasting what God is doing in my personal ministry compared to the ministries of others. When that happens, I will always come up short. I can feel that because I'm not seeing the phenomenal results that others are seeing, something is wrong with me; I need to pray more, maybe I have the wrong strategies and tactics, if only I had more resources (more people, more finances), and the list goes on and on. I begin to equate results with spiritual works that I need to do in order to become more effective. I am to cultivate results through intimate stewardship, but results are grace gifts from God. Ministry results are not the indicator of spiritual intimacy.

The true indicator of spiritual intimacy is experiencing great joy and pleasure in relationship with Christ. Let's look again at Philippians 3:7-8.

> *"But whatever things were gain to me, those things I have counted as loss for the sake of Christ. More than that, I count all things to be loss in view of the surpassing value of knowing Christ Jesus my Lord, for whom I have suffered the loss of all things, and count them but rubbish so that I may gain Christ."*

When we lived in England, we became members of Cranleigh Baptist Church. It was a small church in a quiet village in Surrey. I discovered that some of the first missionaries to China who went with Hudson Taylor (1832 -1905) were from that church. Hudson Taylor spent his first 17 years in China not seeing a single person come to know Christ. He left on furlough to return to England; and in 1865, he wrote in his diary, "For two or three months, intense conflict ... Thought I should lose my mind." A friend invited him to the south coast of England, to Brighton, for a break. It was there, while walking along the beach, that Taylor's gloom lifted:

> "There the Lord conquered my unbelief, and I surrendered myself to God for this service. I told Him that all responsibility as to the issues and consequences must rest with Him; that as His servant, it was mine to obey and to follow Him."

As he returned with new coworkers, they began to see many who came to faith in Christ. The secret to Hudson Taylor's spiritual life was "abiding in Christ." It wasn't an abiding in Christ for the sake of spiritual mission. It was an abiding in Christ no matter what the results.

There is something more important that results in mission with God. It is intimacy with Him. Everything else is compared as loss in view of the purpose of our life in the surpassing value of knowing (experiencing) Christ. Peter (1 Peter 1:8) talks of the personal oneness with God where we greatly rejoice with joy that is inexpressible and full of glory.

Intimacy with Him is of far greater value than mission with Him. The oneness of personal relationship with Him is of greater value to God than the oneness of mission with Him.

The proof of abiding in Him is not ministry results. It is great joy and pleasure in intimate experience of Him.

Phenomenon should be desired and prayed for but not sought after as proof to authenticate relationship with God. Intimacy with God is not based upon phenomenon that He does but upon relationship that is experienced with Him. The scribes and Pharisees believed that works, rather than relationship, were what determined spirituality. They would not accept Christ as God unless He would continually perform works that could be attributed to God. They had no relationship with Christ because relationship with Him was not based upon performance or accomplishment. Phenomenon had to be a way of life for them in order for them to accept Christ as God. Acceptance of Him was devoid of relationship because He had to always perform for them.

> *"Then some of the scribes and Pharisees said to Him, 'Teacher,*
> *we want to see a sign from you.' But He answered and said to*
> *them, 'An evil and adulterous generation craves for a sign; and*
> *yet no sign will be given to it but the sign of JONAH THE PROPHET;*
> *FOR JUST AS JONAH WAS THREE DAYS AND THREE NIGHTS IN THE*
> *BELLY OF THE SEA MONSTER, so shall the Son of Man be three days*
> *and three nights in the heart of the earth.'"* Matthew 12:38-40

What does it mean to be an adulterous generation that seeks after a sign? Adultery is when a marriage partner has sex with someone other than their husband of wife. The basis for the sex is not to cultivate or nourish relationship. It is the performance of sexual gratification from someone outside the marriage bond. The relationship is based upon sexual performance, not the cultivation of a companionship of oneness. An adulterer is someone who has a performance-based sexual relationship outside of marriage.

The seeking of a sign by Christ to authenticate Him as God is like an adulterer thinking sex will give him relationship. Relationship is cultivated and nurtured through intimacy. Intimacy takes place in a bond of oneness that two people of the opposite sex have with each other. Sex, in the intimate bond of oneness, is certainly a part of intimacy. It is the physical sign of the deep bond of intimacy of relationship. But sex, apart from the bond of intimate relationship, is simply a work to be performed. It can be perceived as relationship, but relationship is not based upon performance. Sex, outside of intimate relationship, is performance-based relationship. It is a sign that has to be continually performed in order to prove relationship.

The world's basis for relationship is works that have to be performed. In order to have relationship, one must continually perform well. It is a wicked, perverted way to view relationship.

Simon the magician was confused about this also.

> *"Now there was a man named Simon, who formerly was practicing magic in the city and astonishing the people of Samaria, claiming to be someone great; and they all, from smallest to greatest, were giving attention to him, saying, 'This man is what is called the Great Power of God.'*
>
> *And they were giving him attention because he had for a long time astonished them with his magic arts.*
>
> *But when they believed Philip preaching the good news about the kingdom of God and the name of Jesus Christ, they were being baptized, men and women alike. Even Simon himself believed; and after being baptized, he continued on with Philip, and as he observed signs and great miracles taking place, he was constantly amazed."* Acts 8:9-13
>
> *"Then they began laying their hands on them, and they were receiving the Holy Spirit. Now when Simon saw that the Spirit was bestowed through the laying on of the apostles' hands, he offered them money, saying, 'Give this authority to me as well, so that everyone on whom I lay my hands may receive the Holy Spirit.' But Peter said to him, 'May your silver perish with you, because you thought you could obtain the gift of God with*

money! You have no part or portion in this matter, for your heart
is not right before God. Therefore repent of this wickedness of
yours, and pray the Lord that, if possible, the intention of your
heart may be forgiven you.'" Acts 8:17-22

Simon the magician was a person who claimed greatness because of the
magic he performed. He drew their attention and astonished the people
with his magic. As a believer, he was amazed by the signs and miracles
performed by the disciples. In the first century, the Holy Spirit was
bestowed upon believers through the laying on of the apostles' hands.
Simon was amazed by the authority of the disciples in the laying on of
hands to bestow the Holy Spirit. He offered money in order to have this
authority.

The gift of God was relationship with God that could not be paid for.
What can only be given as a gift cannot be worked for, earned through
performance, or bought with money.

In *Banners of Bonding,* it speaks to the wording "the gift of God."

> The greatest joy and pleasure that we could experience in life is
> relationship with God.

> The Creator of the universe has also created our person. He wants
> us to know and experience bonding and intimacy of relationship
> with Him. We can have and experience relationship with God by
> accepting the free gift of His person.

> Let's look again at Ephesians 2:8-9.

> > *"For by grace you have been saved through faith; and that not of*
> > *yourselves, it is the gift of God; not as a result of works, that no*
> > *one may boast."*

> Relationship with God is the grace gift of God not on the basis
> of works. There are many grace gifts of God, and grace gifting
> is the way that relationship with God is experienced. But there is
> also "the" grace gift of God that is spoken of here. "The grace gift
> of God" is "the grace gift" of His person to our person. It is the

ultimate gift. "The gift" of God is what life is all about. It is the purpose for which we were created – to know and experience God.

Simon was a person who had experienced the attention and amazement of others. His notoriety had come from the works of magic that he performed. It gave him a feeling of authority. When he saw the changed lives experienced through the Holy Spirit, he thought that this was a result of a work that could be performed. He wanted the fame and authority that would come through the performance of this act. His idea was to buy the secret or the power to accomplish this task.

But the power of the Holy Spirit is the grace relationship gift from God. It is the same "the grace gift" of relationship with God that is spoken of in Ephesians 2:8-9. Grace is always a gift and cannot be worked for, earned through performance, or bought with money. Peter asks Simon to repent of his wickedness of trying to experience phenomenon through works or performance.

Phenomenon can be viewed as the way that God is authenticated in our life and mission. It can be viewed as the proof that a person has authority from God. However, to do so is to put God on a works, performance basis. Phenomenon may happen; but when it does, it is a grace gift from God. The joy and pleasure of intimate oneness with God (and not phenomenon) is the proof of intimate relationship and intimate stewardship.

There will be a tendency to view lack of results in mission as a competency that has not been achieved. This is easy to do, particularly when we see or hear of others who are experiencing great results. I am not diminishing the need for equipping in skills and the importance of competency in the accomplishment tasks that will lead to greater effectiveness. I majored in business management and love to plan, organize, and execute strategies.

But seeking phenomenon through hard work and strategies can become a refuge of those who have no intimacy. In many ways, that is a description of much of my first 20 years of mission.

Intimate stewardship of resources may help to cultivate results but is not a guarantee of them.

Upon graduation from college, my first assignment with Cru was the University of Arkansas. I had only been a Christian for three years and still had a lot of personal and spiritual growing ahead of me. I was on a wonderful team who had a vision to win, build, and send students at the U of A.

I soon discovered that not only was I a rookie, but I was on a rookie team. Cru was new at Arkansas, so there was no precedent of previous proven strategies and activities. Everyone on the team was new at Christian ministry, and we were learning what to do from the Lord and each other. There was a lot of trial and error and mistakes. We had no idea what we were doing but loved the Lord, labored as intimate stewards of resources given us, and enjoyed doing mission together.

God did great things those early years. We had speaking and sharing opportunities in all the fraternities and sororities, and in many dorms we were able to share Christ through meetings on each floor. We held weekly meetings of 400 and sometimes larger, and Bible studies were in every housing unit on campus and many apartment complexes. Discipleship was taking place with hundreds of students, and the campus was blanketed with literature with attractive articles and testimonies about how to know Christ. Athletes from many different teams came to know Christ and were a part of our leadership training. One summer, 70 students spent 10 weeks in Biblical training at our headquarters. There were several years when around 20 students joined Cru full-time upon graduation. There truly was a revival and awakening at the University of Arkansas in the early 70s that was experienced not just by us, but by many other student ministries and churches.

Our team was continually amazed at the results that we were seeing. The results were far greater than our competencies at ministry. God was moving, and we were privileged to be a part of it. But we also realized that what God was doing was in spite of us, not because of us.

That movement of God at the University of Arkansas lasted for about three years.

I learned in my early years that results are in the Lord's hands. No amount of competency, giftedness, strategy, and effective results will be a substitute for what God does through His grace. It is easy to stray from the priority of intimacy with Him and seek phenomenon as proof of authority we have with Him. When there seems to be lack of results, there will be a tendency to work harder in order to justify who we are and what we do. Accomplishments will be become a refuge for us because of our lack of intimacy with God.

Life will become wearisome and performance-driven.

Grace gifting of phenomenon is not just related to Christian mission. It is true of any mission/vocation. Gifted surgeons will go bankrupt through questionable lawsuits. Natural disasters will destroy property and businesses. People will lose jobs in economic downturns. Industries will be eliminated through technology and innovation. A lifetime of faithful saving can be taken away through inflation. Intimate stewardship of resources is not necessarily a guarantee of the desired outcome.

Likewise, a person can see financial phenomenon without necessarily the accompanying effort. Employees of Wal-Mart, at its beginning, who invested in stock through their incomes, became millionaires over time. In the early 20th century, people amassed fortunes simply because there were valuable minerals discovered on property they owned.

Recently, my son, Edward, met a friend that he knew from high school. His friend had developed a security company that had become international in scope. At age 27, he sold the company for millions of dollars.

Joy and pleasure will be experienced when we are involved in mission with God as intimate stewards of resources, cultivating results, but realizing that any results are grace gifts from God. We are to seek God and not results that He gives. Phenomenon may happen, but it will always be a grace gift from God.

Closing Thoughts on the Boundary of Intimate Stewardship of Resources

Intimate stewardship of resources can only take place when intimacy with God is the purpose of our life and our mission in life is to be one with Him in the destiny that He has for us. There is a great commandment (Matthew 22:35-37) and a great commission (Matthew 28:18-20) that God has for all of us. The great commandment is always a priority over the great commission. They both form a basis of oneness (unity) with God that is the dream that He has for us. In this context of oneness with God, there are great benefits of the intimate stewardship of resources.

We have a shared joy with God. We looked at this earlier when we examined that our view of God determines our stewardship. In the parable of the talents (Matthew 25:14-30), the master speaks of the joy and pleasure that the faithful stewards experience with Him (25:21, 23). They are actually able to enjoy the same pleasure that the Lord Himself enjoys. It is the joy of oneness in the doing of good works.

We experience an intimate oneness with God. We are intimate stewards of the resources God gives us and recognize that results are grace gifts from Him. We no longer need to perform for Him in order to have results that excel. Our responsibility is to be an intimate steward of resources. The quality of the result is God's responsibility, and we are grateful for whatever results the Lord provides. We must understand that God values the oneness of intimacy with Him in the stewardship of His resources as more important than the results that are produced. Results are grace gifts from Him. Whatever the results, we can experience oneness with God. Oneness (abiding, unity, intimacy) is the purpose of God's creation of us. It is the highest value of God for us.

Our life has purpose and meaning. In John 10:10, Jesus talks about the abundant life: "The thief comes only to steal and kill and destroy; I came that they may have life, and have it abundantly." The world offers many formulas for success, but they all involve works, performance, and obligation. The focus is upon self. Domination, control, and manipulation are the methods. Comparison, competition, rivalries, and jealousies are the results. They are devoid of intimacy, grace, and relationship. They steal purpose and meaning in life from us.

Purpose and meaning in life are only found in intimate relationship with God. When our life is surrendered to Christ and we desire to reflect who He is in our person, then, and only then, will life personally and emotionally make sense. The Greek word used for the abundant life is *zoe*. It refers to a quality experience of life. It is the life that Adam and Eve experienced in the Garden of Eden before they sinned. Genesis 1:26 it says, "Let Us make man in Our image, according to Our likeness." "According to Our likeness" refers to the life they lived that was experienced completely in the context of intimate relationship with God. It was the purpose of their creation. Just because sin entered the world, it did not change the original intention of God's creation of us. Intimacy with Him has always been, and always will be, where we experience purpose and meaning in life.

Intimate stewardship of resources is the alignment of our destiny with the destiny that God has for us. He leads, guides, and directs us in the way in which we should go. He counsels us with His eye upon us (Psalm 32:8). His plan for the ages (the redemption of mankind unto Himself) becomes our plan through the intimate stewardship of resources. How that destiny unfurls for each of us will be different but no less important. It is the intimacy of oneness with Him in person and in destiny through which we experience purpose and meaning to life.

The boundary of intimate stewardship of resources is essential to the cultivation of relationship with God. We can have relationship with God but not truly experience Him. We can receive the gift of God (eternal life) but direct and control our own destinies apart from God. We can labor for God apart from oneness with Him. Stewardship only makes sense when it is intimate with God. Mission can focus upon self. It can focus upon godly activities. But God's creation of us is for mission to be one with Him in the doing together of the good works He has for us.

There will be the tendency to over-invest in mission because we believe that results are what are most important. However, there is always something more important than results – it is intimacy with God! And there is something more important than the good works of mission for God – it is the oneness of mission with Him!

In the oneness of mission with Him, we are responsible to be good stewards of the resources God has given us: competencies, relationships (manpower), finances, and time. We are to cultivate results, always aware that results are grace gifts from God. When we overinvest in results, we go beyond good stewardship and intimate oneness of mission with God. Results then become a greater priority than intimacy with God, and eventually our life and our mission become works and obligations that have to be performed.

The opposite can also happen. Instead of overinvesting in mission, we check out of it. We decide just to do our own thing. Some people decide to do nothing. Because mission (vocation) is confusing and results have been elusive, they decide to no longer be responsible vocationally and they do nothing. It is the opposite of overinvesting in stewardship.

We can fool ourselves to believe that we have intimacy with God without mission with Him, but a branch that abides in a vine bears fruit (John 15:5). To be one with Him will result in the world knowing that God sent Jesus and loves the world as God loves His Son (John 17:23). If we love God with all out heart, soul, and mind, then we will love our neighbor as our self (Matthew 22:39). Intimacy as mission will result when we experience the priority of intimacy with God. For intimacy as mission to be absent is to be a poor steward.

Just as Adam was given the responsibilities to cultivate and keep (protect) the Garden of Eden, so we are to cultivate relationship with God through keeping the boundary of the intimate stewardship of resources. As the Garden of Eden was a walled enclosure where joy and pleasure was experienced, so the intimate stewardship of resources protects the greatest joy and pleasure that can be experienced in life – intimacy with God.

Discussion Questions

1. Share a personal story of phenomenon in your life. How did it relate to the grace of God?

2. In what ways are you experiencing your destiny (what you do) aligned with the destiny God has for you? Share specifics.

3. Why is intimacy with God always a greater priority than intimate stewardship with Him?

Work is
an investment
in accomplishment.
Rest is
the investment
in person
(relationship).

For in six days
the LORD *made the heavens*
and the earth, the sea and all that is in them,
and rested on the seventh day;
therefore the LORD *blessed*
the sabbath day and
made it holy.

Exodus 20:11

THE CRUCIAL BOUNDARY OF REST

I. God's Rest

The fourth boundary that cultivates bonding with God is the crucial boundary of rest. We need to take a close look at a definition of rest. Genesis 2:2-3 is the first mention of rest in the Bible.

> *"By the seventh day God completed His work which He had done, and He rested on the seventh day from all His work which He had done. God blessed the seventh day and sanctified it, because in it He rested from all His work which God had created and made."*

The Hebrew word for rest is *shabath*. It is from this root that the noun Sabbath originates. Sabbath refers to the length of the rest, a Sabbath rest, the rest that is a day in length. The rest in this passage refers to God's rest at the end of the work that was His creation.

The obvious reference to rest is the cessation of work. But we must ask the question, "Why does God who has no need of rest choose to do so?" God does not grow weary or become tired. Rest has much more to it than just a physical rest from work.

Work is an investment in accomplishment. We have already examined the role of work as the intimate stewardship of resources. Our responsibility is to be a good steward that cultivates results. It is vital to understand that we are one with the Lord (intimate) in the doing of the good works that He has for us (Ephesians 2:10), and results are His responsibility (grace gifts).

Rest is the cessation of investment in accomplishment. It is the investment in person (relationship). When God rested, He intentionally ceased His investment in His creation; and He chose to invest in His person (the Trinity). He values investment in relationship as greater than investment in accomplishment, and rest is the demonstration of the value that God places upon intimacy with Him (the Trinity with each other). After God's creative project of the universe, the world, the land and the waters, the vegetation and the animals, and finally the creation of mankind, He chose to rest. The Trinity intentionally rested in the great joy and pleasure they experienced with each other after they had experienced the oneness of the intimate stewardship of creation.

Why does God, who has no need of rest, choose to do so?

Why do we, who are so desperately in need of rest, refuse to do so?

He invests in oneness of creation and oneness of relationship. He intentionally chooses to rest because He values relationship with Him as of greater value than accomplishment with Him. We can tend to overinvest in being stewards that cultivate results and intentionally not rest because we value results over relationships.

Rest for us should be an intentional investment in person (relationship). There is not a formula for rest, but it is not a continuing of works or performance. Let's look at some other input on rest.

II. Sabbath Rest

The second mention of rest in the Bible is in the Ten Commandments given to Moses. It talks of a Sabbath day of rest.

> *"Remember the Sabbath day, to keep it holy. Six day you shall labor and do all your work, but the seventh day is a Sabbath of the LORD your God; in it you shall not do any work, you or your son or your daughter, your male or your female servant or your cattle or your sojourner who stays with you. For in six days the LORD made the heavens and the earth, the sea and all that is in*

them, and rested on the seventh day; therefore the LORD blessed
the Sabbath day and made it holy." Exodus 20:8-11

This passage says the Sabbath day is to be without work, not just for us but also for our family. Employees should cease laboring on Sunday. Guests staying with us should not work on the Sabbath. The Sabbath was to be a holy day. It was to be a holy rest.

When we think of holiness, there are two thoughts that usually come to mind. There is holiness that is pure, glorious, and perfection. For most people, holiness is separateness, seclusion from the world, isolation from temptation, and an aloofness from others. Holiness tends to be perceived as anti-pleasure. Let me share some thoughts from *Banners of Bonding*.

In the introduction, we looked at holiness as seeming to be a list of rules and regulations to follow. It feels like anti-pleasure. I have heard of holy men and women in Christian history and of other religions. Many were people who isolated themselves from others for the purpose of being closer to God. They were disciplined in actions that were supposed to produce godliness. Even though their deeds might have seemed commendable, they had lifestyles that most people would not deem desirable. Holiness seems elusive.

And yet we are called to be holy.

"But like the Holy One who called you, be holy yourselves also in
all your behavior; because it is written, 'YOU SHALL BE HOLY, FOR
I AM HOLY.'" 1 Peter 1:15-16

"Just as He chose us in Him before the foundation of the world,
that we would be holy and blameless before Him."
Ephesians 1:4

"And although you were formally alienated and hostile in mind,
engaged in evil deeds, yet He has now reconciled you in His
fleshly body through death, in order to present you before Him
holy and blameless and above reproach." Colossians 1:21-22

How then is holiness to be defined? How does holiness relate to God? What does holiness require of us?

Holiness is the foremost attribute of God that makes sure intimacy is honored. Holiness characterizes the relationship the Trinity experiences with each other. God the Father – God the Son – and God the Holy Spirit so value intimacy of their persons that they will not allow the richness of joy and pleasure that they experience with each other to be ever be broken. God, who is one in essence but three in person, seeks relational glory through holiness of person. Each member of the Godhead will establish boundaries (or say "no") to anything that would take away from the oneness (bonding, abiding, intimacy) that they have with each other. Holiness assures that ultimate pleasure and joy will be experienced by the members of the Trinity.

When God says, "You shall be holy as I am holy," He means that we should establish boundaries around (or say "no" to) anything that would prevent greater oneness, deeper bonding, fuller abiding, and richer intimacy with Him.

I have a friend who is a recovering alcoholic. What was once a simple pleasure in his life, a glass of wine at the evening meal, became an addiction to alcohol as a way to provide comfort and escape from the problems of his life. His addiction became an issue in his marriage, his work, and eventually his friendships. His life was being destroyed by alcohol, which was at one time a simple pleasure. It had become an obsession.

Through caring friends, he began to realize that he was destroying everything that was important to him. He joined Alcoholics Anonymous and began to admit his addiction. He has a sponsor that was in touch with him daily to help him no longer drink alcohol. Over time, he began to see victory over his addiction, and he became a sponsor to others who needed help.

In the midst of this process, he sought help from a higher power. A pastor shared with Him the abundant life that could be found in

Christ. He received Jesus Christ for the forgiveness of his sins and surrendered his life to Him.

The joy and pleasure of a life in oneness with God began to fill his heart. Relationship and fellowship with God became his greatest pleasure. Intimacy with God became his passion in life.

His desire was to allow nothing to prevent him from the joy, pleasure, and abundance of life he now had in Christ. Alcohol, even though it was still a constant temptation, had been replaced by relational intimacy with God and others.

> *"You have put gladness in my heart,*
> *More than when their grain and new wine abound.*
>
> *In peace I will both lie down and sleep,*
> *For you alone, Lord, make me to dwell in safety."*
> Psalm 4:7-8

Holiness is not a list of do's and don'ts. It is not rules and regulations to follow. It is a wonderful, deep, intimate relationship with God that does not allow anyone or anything to take away from it.

Holiness is not isolation from the world but a set apartness to God in togetherness with Him. It is held firm in a bond that refuses to be broken.

Holiness is not anti-pleasure. It is the setting of boundaries (or saying "no") to anything that would prevent deep intimacy with God. In this respect, holiness manages pleasure and makes it safe because God knows the appropriateness of pleasure that we need. When we pursue the greatest joy and pleasure in life (which is the richness of intimacy we have with God) and establish boundaries around anything that would prevent that, then we are pursuing holiness. We can be holy if we are willing to let pleasure be managed by the choice of deep intimacy with God.

Without holiness, pleasure-seeking will destroy intimacy with God.

Holiness, putting boundaries around anything that would prevent intimacy
with God, assures that we will experience the greatest joy and pleasure
in life – intimacy with God. Intimacy with God is not a work to be
accomplished but a relationship to be experienced. Intentional investment
in relationship with God and others can be characterized as rest. It is well
stated in Matthew 11:28-30.

> *"Come to me, all who are weary and heavy-laden, and I will
> give you rest. Take My yoke upon you and learn from Me, for
> I am gentle and humble in heart, and* YOU WILL FIND REST FOR
> YOUR SOULS. *For My yoke is easy and My burden is light."*

Rest is found in relationship. God's yoke is not one of performance that
is weary and heavy. It is learning from Him, who is gentle and humble in
heart. In Him we find rest for our souls.

When God says, "Keep the Sabbath holy," He is telling us to be intentional
in investing time in relationship with God, our self, and others. This time
investment in relationship should not be works, performance, or obligation.
Being with others who desire intimacy with God by going to church on
Sunday can be a great joy and pleasure. However, church attendance can
become an obligation – a duty we have to perform each week in order to
be spiritual. When relationship with God becomes a duty to be performed,
there is no rest for our souls.

Jesus was confronted by the Pharisees about working on the Sabbath.

> *"And it happened that He was passing through the grainfields
> on the Sabbath, and His disciples began to make their way along
> while picking the heads of grain.*
>
> *The Pharisees were saying to Him, 'Look, why are they doing
> what is not lawful on the Sabbath?'*
>
> *And He said to them, 'Have you never read what David did
> when he was in need and he and his companions became
> hungry; how he entered the house of God in the time of
> Abiathar the high priest, and ate the consecrated bread, which is*

not lawful for anyone to eat except the priests, and he also gave it to those who were with him?'

Jesus said to them, 'The Sabbath was made for man, and not man for the Sabbath. So the Son of Man is Lord even of the Sabbath.

He entered again into a synagogue; and a man was there whose hand was withered. They were watching Him to see if He would heal him on the Sabbath, so that they might accuse Him. He said to the man with the withered hand, 'Get up and come forward!' And He said to them, 'Is it lawful to do good or to do harm on the Sabbath, to save a life or to kill?' But they kept silent.

After looking around at them with anger, grieved at their hardness of heart, He said to the man, 'Stretch out your hand.' And he stretched it out, and his hand was restored.

The Pharisees went out and immediately began conspiring with the Herodians against Him, as to how they might destroy Him."
Mark 2:23-3:6

The Pharisees were a religious cult that believed that spirituality was based upon works. They followed the Ten Commandments and the centuries of additions to it known as the Jewish law. They confronted Jesus about gathering grain on the Sabbath. They felt this should be defined as work and therefore could not take place on the Sabbath because the law said that no work could be done on the Sabbath. The Sabbath was to be observed as a holy day of rest. Any work was not to take away from the intentional priority of intimacy with God. Jesus, who was the Son of Man, told them that the Sabbath was made for man, not man for the Sabbath. In other words, Jesus created the Sabbath. He understood how important rest was and how it related to investment in relationship with Him. To pick grain to satisfy hunger and to heal on the Sabbath did not violate the principle of rest. The Pharisees were angered by this because Jesus seemed to not be playing by their rules. Rest to the Pharisees involved conduct, performance, and works to which one must abstain. But Sabbath rest had always been for the purpose of intentionally cultivating and nourishing relationship.

Holiness is the key to Sabbath rest. It is a day when work is set aside to focus upon not allowing anything to prevent intimacy with God as the purpose of our life.

III. Believer's Rest

There is a third mention of rest in the Bible that is described as the believer's rest.

> *"So there remains a Sabbath rest for the people of God. For the one who has entered His rest has himself also rested from his works, as God did from His."* Hebrews 4:9-10

This is a beautiful description of the eternal life relationship of the believer in Christ. Salvation is by grace through faith. There is nothing we can do to earn what can only be given as a gift. We can only rest in the sufficiency of God's grace gift of relationship with Him through the death of Jesus Christ on the cross for our sins. We cannot purchase through our hard work that which is priceless and can only be received as a gift. We must cease from our own efforts, our striving, our performance and rest in receiving what only God can do.

Sabbath rest is compared to the believer's rest in the grace gift of relationship with God. Rest is the intentional investment in relationship with God. It involves no work on our part. It is the resting in relationship with God that is likened to the absolute rest or cessation of activity or labor done by us to establish relationship with God.

The theme of the book of Ecclesiastes is emptiness or vanity. "No profit under the sun" and "vanity and striving after wind" are several expressions used in the book to communicate the futility and meaninglessness of life apart from intimacy with God.

Ecclesiastes 4:4-6 talks about the relationship between labor and rest.

> *"I have seen that every labor and every skill which is done is the result of rivalry between a man and his neighbor. This too is vanity and striving after wind.*
>
> *The fool folds his hands and consumes his own flesh.*
>
> *One hand full of rest is better than two fists full of labor and striving after wind."*

This passage talks about labor as a form of comparison, competition, and rivalry. Results and the competition involved in besting others can, for many people, become an obsession. Work can literally become the driving force in a person's life. They define who they are by what they do and how that compares with others.

It says that the fool folds his hands and does nothing (consumes his own flesh). Some people look at labor and decide to not engage in it. They see labor as useless or senseless and are passive toward it. They are trusting others to take care of them. Labor has value and is necessary, but it is not the purpose of life. Those who choose to not labor are referred to as fools.

There is a comparison between a hand full and a fist full. A hand full refers to a hand that can carry the largest amount. The fingers and thumb are cupped and joined. The hand is open and relaxed. A fist full refers to a hand that allows little to escape. This closed hand contains an amount that is tightly clenched.

Some people's lives are like two closed, tightened, clenched fists. Labor is their life and there is no room for rest. Their life is invested in accomplishment. Performance to obtain greater results consumes them. The lack of rest is an indicator that accomplishment must be done through them. The harder they work, the greater should be the results. Results, for them, are not grace gifts from God, but entitlements to be received from their tireless and endless performance at accomplishment. Rest is rarely an option because results are up to them, and achievement is more important than relationships. Their lives are characterized by striving after wind.

However, there are people who have one hand full of rest and one fist full of labor. This is the appropriate emphasis between labor and rest; intimacy with God (hand full-relationship-rest) and labor for Him (fist full-mission-labor). Rest is essential to intimacy with God, which is the priority of life. When rest is absent, then we reflect that accomplishment is more important than relationship.

God highly values rest. Investment in person and relationship are of great importance to Him. His priority is relationship over accomplishment. Grace is superior to works. Intimacy with Him is a greater priority than service for Him. He has designed who we are as more important than what we do.

God desires that we highly value rest. It is an investment in relationship with God, our self, and others. Our priority should be relationship over accomplishment. Grace should be superior to works. Intimacy with God ought to be a greater priority for us than our other desires and pleasure.

When we do not highly value rest, then we find ourselves prioritizing accomplishment over relationship, works as superior to grace, service for God a greater priority than intimacy with Him, and what we do as more important than who we are. In our heart, soul, mind, and body, there will be no rest.

IV. A Temporary Disclaimer to Physical Rest

Intimacy with God will always be the priority over mission with God. However, there can be temporary, infrequent times in which physical rest can appropriately be set aside.

I have a friend who owns a bread company. His sales in November and December are larger than the rest of the year combined. The workload for those two months can be massive.

A student who attended a leadership training center that I was directing many years ago gave up his fireworks franchise in order to be a part of this spiritual emphasis. He had previously earned enough during two months of work each summer to finance his college education. He worked day and night during those two months.

Last April, I met a gentleman who has a business selling fruit baskets each fall that focus upon sales for Christmas gifts. His entire income was determined in how well he was prepared to sell and ship his product in a six-week period.

In campus ministry, everyone knows that the first six weeks of the school year will determine your results the rest of the year.

There are times when we as a nation are at war. Men and women leave families and friends to be gone up to a year in another part of the world. Their sacrifices are great: poor living conditions, long and enduring schedules, dangerous assignments, and possibility of wounding or death.

There are times in our lives when we must go for it. Physical rest is not an option. For a specific period of time, we have to give all we have. A year's worth of sales that happen in a brief period of time cannot be entered into casually. The first six weeks of campus ministry are an endurance in order for the rest of the school year to be maximized. Wars are not fought and won in leisurely ways.

However, there are two factors that are necessary in order for physical rest to be temporarily set aside. **The first is that your key relationships in life that will be involved in the results of setting aside physical rest are in agreement with your decision.** This decision has been processed with God, and you believe that you are one with Him in the good works that you will be doing. You brought together your relational value base of family, covenant team members, kingdom citizen relationships, and possibly other close friendships and have their blessing upon the decision. Those key relationships in life that are more important to you than what you accomplish are in agreement with the work you have to do that will temporarily set aside physical rest.

Those involved in the accomplishment of the work with you must also agree to its priority and appropriateness. Peers, co-laborers, employees, associates, and your team are in agreement that the work you are doing involves the setting aside of physical rest.

The second factor is that the setting aside of physical rest is a temporary setting aside. It is intended for a specific period of time. The disclaimer of the setting aside of physical rest must be temporary because such great risk is involved. If the setting aside of physical rest goes beyond a temporary, specific set time for its cessation, then there is the potential that accomplishment becomes more important than relationship, works as superior to grace, service for God a greater priority than intimacy with Him, and what we do as more important than who we are.

Both of these factors are necessary in order to enter into the disclaimer.

If these factors are not present or they are violated, then what was intended to be a temporary priority will become a way of life. An unhealthy sense of drivenness that does not allow for physical rest will begin to characterize our life. Over time, there will become a weariness, tiredness, and burdensome feeling about life. Eventually, our lives will experience what is known as a burnout. It comes from a life invested in accomplishment that is devoid of relationship.

It is also important to realize that when we set aside a boundary that allows physical rest to be appropriate that relational rest with God, self, and others is still a priority. However, in times of increased physical activity our relational rest may also look different. It may not be as scheduled, as lengthy or as familiar.

My wife, Beth, has been approached many times for advice from mothers of toddlers having difficulty in aloneness time with God like they did before they had children. Her encouragement to them is to take advantage of any opportunity that arises. Even though they live with physical exhaustion from caring for their children, there can be five minutes of time to pray or read just a portion of scripture. Sometimes God will give them a special grace gift of a few moments to cultivate their relationship with Him in the midst of demanding physical activity.

My ministry involves periodic times of travel. The next two and a half weeks are an incredibly busy travel time for me. I have known this for several months. There are six activities that I am directing that are back-to-back over the next eighteen days. There was an earlier time in my life in which I would have immediately said "yes" to these activities because they were challenging and enjoyable. However, at this phase of my life, before saying "yes" to these, I really prayed about their importance and my need to be involved. There is not a compulsion to have to do any of these activities. The Lord has given me a "go for it" attitude that does not involve my success being wrapped up in these events. I have discussed it with Beth and what she feels would be best. She is able to be with me on several of these, and that is a high priority in my acceptance.

I have asked my friends Ed, Bill, Baldwin, and Hal for their input. They are in agreement with me as to the use of the time and as to the temporary nature of the events. We will talk shortly after the time is over, and there are questions that we will discuss to make sure that I have not left the boundary of the intimate stewardship of resources and the boundary of rest. Here are the questions we will discuss:

- Was what I did enjoyable (as opposed to a duty or obligation)?

- Did I associate my success by the results I saw? (Would a good result make me feel more significant? Would a poor result cause me to feel less significant?)

- Did I do these activities to comfort myself? (Were there other things I was trying to avoid by going on this trip?)

- Did I confuse my priorities? (Even though this was a "disclaimer time" to set aside physical rest, was I sensitive to opportunities to connect with the Lord and minister to others?)

I already have in my schedule some time for rest once the temporary priority of good works are accomplished.

This is the way it works for me. You might say, "David, that is a lot of work (checking with God and others) to insure that you don't overinvest in performance that becomes a way of life." But you need to understand that I am a recovering workaholic. I spent my first twenty years of ministry overinvesting in results at the expense of relationships. I cannot go back to that way of life, even though I could easily do so. I am experiencing a joy and pleasure in God and others that is affirming, strengthening, and empowering. Becoming an intimate steward of resources that recognizes the crucial boundary of rest has been an ongoing journey for me. It has also become a great relief.

Genuine emotional and personal strength in life comes from relationships. Our relationships can certainly be challenging, but they are what support and encourage our person (who we are). Relationship with God is the ultimate strength and affirmation there is in life. Performance in accomplishment of goals holds no comparison to investment in relationship with Him and who we are (our identity) in Him.

When we overinvest in accomplishment, the boundary of rest (that assures intimacy with God) will be violated. There are specific consequences that are results when we do not honor the boundary of rest:

- You develop an unhealthy sense of drivenness to prove who you are by what you do.

- Work and ministry becomes an obligation or duty.

- You can develop an entitlement mindset that you are owed something (manpower, finances, and time).

- Life becomes works / performance related, rather than grace / relationship experienced.

- You become critical of those in leadership and even critical of God. Those in leadership are viewed as dominating and demanding.

- There is no joy.

- There is no rest for your soul.

- You lose your first love (intimacy with God).

- You burn out emotionally, physically, and spiritually.

It is deeply saddening to see someone who has set aside the boundary of physical rest to go beyond good stewardship in the accomplishing of results. I am not talking about a casual approach to work or laziness that tries to get out of working hard. I am referring to a worker that is worthy of his labor: faithful, diligent, conscientious, and responsible. However, that worker has gone beyond good stewardship and fails to see that results are grace gifts from God.

I am around men almost daily who have overinvested in accomplishment at the expense of relationship. It is a particular malaise of men in their thirties. They feel that if they are ever going to succeed vocationally, it must happen before age forty. If they don't, then they feel they will be overlooked and passed by. However, they also experience the emotion of wanting to have greater security than ever before. The security comes from relationships (God, their wife, their family covenant relationships of the same gender, church, community) not from vocation. They seem trapped between these two competing emotions (success and security), and there is not enough time to do both.

As a person ages, it becomes more apparent that relationship is of greater value than accomplishment; but for some people, this realization is hard for them to accept. Accomplishment is where they have invested their life, and it is an insatiable exploit that consumes them. Comparison, competition, and obligation are the daily emotions they face. Entitlement because of their hard work becomes the expression of their person. We all know people like this, at the end of their lives, who are bitter, angry, and unpleasant to be around.

Rest is relational. It is an investment in our person and covenant relationships with others. Ultimately rest is found in a deep, bonded relationship with God. Jesus makes this clear in Matthew 11:28-30.

> *"Come to Me, all who are weary and heavy-laden, and I will give you rest. Take My yoke upon you and learn from Me, for I am gentle and humble in heart, and* YOU WILL FIND REST FOR YOUR SOULS. *For My yoke is easy and My burden is light."*

Jesus bids us to come to Him for rest. As we come to Him and learn from Him, we find Him gentle with a heart that is humble. The burdens and weariness of life, when given to Him, become a load that is light because of the relationship we experience in Him. It is not simply the exchange of our burdens for His lighter load. It is the rest we have in Him that comes from personally experiencing who He is (gentle, humble in heart) and Him experiencing who we are. It is this oneness of purpose, this intimacy with God, which transcends all the circumstances of life and allows us to experience the greatest joy and pleasure that exists. We are able to rest in Him. Intimacy with God is the purpose of our creation by God. When we rest in Him, He experiences great joy and pleasure in us. It is a relational glory that we can mutually experience. Part of the glory is experiencing the rest, which is crucial to intimacy with God.

Discussion Questions

1. Why is rest so important to God? Why do we treat it so casually?

2. Why is it easy to set aside the crucial boundary of rest to go beyond good stewardship in the accomplishing of results?

3. What negative effects happen when work in which you are involved, that was agreed to by covenant relationships with a time limit applied, goes beyond the time limit and becomes a vocational way of life?

4. What is a hand full of rest for you?

5. What must you do differently in order to experience a hand full of rest?

We were created to experience an intimate relationship with God.

The glory which You have given Me
I have given to them, that they may be one,
just as We are one; I in them and You in Me,
that they may be perfected in unity…

John 17:22-23a

Closing

Let's review what we have previously examined.

God placed Adam in the beautiful and magnificent Garden of Eden.
Later, Eve was created there to also enjoy its splendor. God gave Adam
the responsibility to cultivate the garden, but more importantly, it was the
place where relationship with God was cultivated. The experiencing of the
intimate relationship with God was the purpose for the creation of Adam
and Eve. For growth and maturity in their relationship, there needed to
be complete dependence upon God and intentional cultivation of that
relationship.

But sin entered the world through the passivity and disobedience of Adam.
Sin had a deep and profound impact upon relationship with God. Some
of the personal effects of sin were isolation from God, an independent
spirit of self-will, and a focus upon self. Some relational effects of sin
were an alienation from God, confusion about one's own identity,
and dysfunctional relationships with others. Intimacy was no longer
experienced, and isolation and alienation were what now characterized the
relationship.

There was nothing Adam and Eve could do to restore their relationships
with God. But, God in His grace provided a way for reconciliation to take
place. It was through the offering of His Son, Jesus Christ, by His death on
the cross as a just provision for our sin.

> *"He made Him who knew no sin to be sin on our behalf, so that
> we might become the righteousness of God in Him."*
> 2 Corinthians 5:21

We have inherited that sin nature from Adam.

> *"All of us like sheep have gone astray, each of us has turned to
> his own way; but the Lord has caused the iniquity of us all to
> fall on Him."* Isaiah 53:6

God gave humanity the grace gift of an eternal life relationship with Him.

> *"For God so loved the world, that He gave His only begotten*
> *Son, that whoever believes in Him shall not perish, but have*
> *eternal life."* John 3:16

When we receive Christ for the forgiveness of our sins, relationship with God is restored. God does, through His grace, what we could never do through our own best works. Grace is how we come to know God, and grace is always the way in which He relates to us. Grace, relationship, truth, bonding and beauty are how the kingdom of God manifests itself.

Just because sin entered the world, it did not change the original intention for God's creation of us. This grace gift of intimate relationship with God is, and always has been, the purpose of life.

Sin is always trying to make relationship with God into a performance for Him. It makes relationship into works to be performed in order to be accepted by God. Sin also makes relationship into duties to be accomplished in order to receive something from God.

So, how do we cultivate intimacy with God? How do we receive and grow in the priceless grace gift with God without making it works or a performance to be accomplished?

Intimate relationship with God involves talking with Him, attentively listening to Him, intelligently hearing from Him, and learning of Him (from His Word). It involves trusting in Him and depending upon Him. It is living all of life in the context of oneness with God where He leads, guides, and directs us in the way in which we should go.

Several times, we have examined the great commandment that defines intimacy or relationship with God found in Matthew 22:35-38. Jesus is talking with the Pharisees who believed relationship with God was determined through spiritual works. The greatest person among them was the one who could best live the Jewish law. Spirituality involved comparison, competition, and obligation. A lawyer among the Pharisees asked Jesus this question,

"Teacher, which is the greatest commandment in the Law?"

Jesus' reply was,

"'YOU SHALL LOVE THE LORD YOUR GOD WITH ALL YOUR HEART, AND WITH ALL YOUR SOUL, AND WITH ALL YOUR MIND.' This is the great and foremost commandment."

Jesus said that spirituality was defined by a relationship to be experienced and not by spiritual works to be accomplished. This passage shares that relationship is experienced in a love relationship with God where our hearts, souls, and minds are as one.

Our heart is where vision, adventure, and passion reside. It is the emotional center of our person. It is our heart that empowers us through the Holy Spirit within us. The essence of our heart is what we surrender our person to, for good or for bad. For our heart to be bonded to the heart of God involves the full surrender of our heart to Him. That full surrender is certainly at a moment in time, but it is also the daily surrender in which we affirm to God that He is our vision and passion in life. No person and no thing will ever empower us the way intimacy experienced with God can do. To have intimacy with God involves the full surrender of our hearts to Him every moment of our lives.

When we speak of our soul, we are talking about where we have determined the value and worth of our person. It is where our identity is formed and nourished. When our soul is bonded to the soul of God, then our value, worth, and identity are aligned to the value, worth, and identity of who God believes us to be. Our true identity is in Him, and He says that we are:

Unique, special, and of high value to Him.

Deeply loved.

Completely accepted.

Totally forgiven.

God is for us and not against us.

Relational intimacy with God in our soul is defined as believing these truths. Our actions and beliefs about ourselves are firmly rooted in the identity of who God says we are.

Our mind is where knowledge and intellect are located. It is also where beauty and truth are experienced. Our competencies are located in our mind. Competencies are ways is which we relate to effectiveness through gifts, skills, and abilities. They also relate to how we process information.

The main aspect of our mind as to how we experience intimacy with God is centered in direction. It is the mind that directs our person. We tend to think of direction as something that is linear or determined through principles. For many people, direction is secret information that God possesses that we must work hard through prayer and study in the Word to discover. However, the key to experiencing intimacy of mind with God is that the foundation of direction is relational, not in a formula or series of determined steps.

Simply put, our mind, bonded to the mind of God, is to be Christ's companion and going in the direction in which He is going. When our directional foundation is to be Christ's companion and to go where He leads, guides, and directs, then He uses His Word, sound mind principles, and the advice of godly friends. He also directs us through the wisdom of others and the leading of the Holy Spirit to direct us from the solid foundation of His mind becoming our mind. True direction in life is centered in the intimacy of our relationship with God where He is the way, the truth, the life, and the light.

Intimacy is defined relationally as:

- The full surrender of our heart to God for today and for all of eternity.

- Believing that we are unique, special, and of high value to God, deeply loved, completely accepted, totally forgiven. God is for us and not against us.

- Being Christ's companion and going in the direction in which He is going.

When these descriptions of intimacy with God are present within our lives, then we are experiencing the greatest joy and pleasure there is in life. Jesus said in John 10:10,

"I came that they may have life, and have it abundantly."

Obviously, there are practical ways that intimacy is expressed through prayer, Bible study, and fellowship with others who pursue intimacy with God as the purpose of life. However, these activities can easily become works we do in order to be spiritual. The bonding of our heart, soul, and mind to the heart, soul, and mind of God is not an activity we do but a relationship that we experience.

Intimacy cannot take place in isolation. A necessity of intimacy with God is bonded covenant relationships with others. We need others in our life who relate to us in the ways in which God relates to us. Experiencing relationships described as "iron sharpens iron, so one man sharpens another" (Proverbs 27:17) and "friends that stick (bond) closer than a brother" (Proverbs 18:24) help us to relate to God who is unseen. God never intended for us to experience intimacy with Him in the context of just Him and us. Bonding with covenant relationships deepens the intimacy we experience with God and helps us to have relational accountability in pursuing intimacy with God for a lifetime.

Adam also had responsibility to keep (protect) the garden. It involved maintaining and protecting the boundary that surrounded the garden. The boundary was necessary in order to for the garden to be well cultivated. The boundary enabled the circumstances and the environment of the garden to be such that fruitfulness might take place. Boundaries are necessary in order for intimacy with God to be cultivated and fruitful. In this study we have looked at the four boundaries that strengthen the eternal bond with God:

Intimacy with God as the Purpose of Life

Intimacy as Mission with God

Intimate Stewardship of Resources

The Crucial Boundary of Rest

It is our responsibility to insure that these boundaries are established and kept. If this is not done, then the cultivation of intimacy with God will become difficult and may not be experienced.

What does it mean in a practical sense to keep the boundaries of intimacy with God? Here is a process that I use that helps me to be focused upon key principles of experiencing the eternal bond with God.

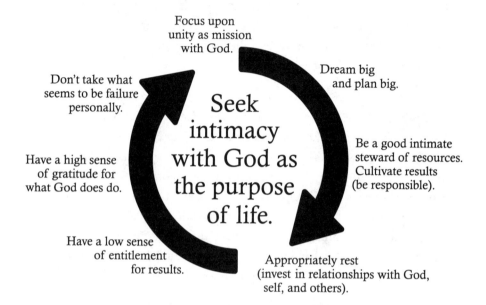

Focus upon unity as mission with God.

Dream big and plan big.

Don't take what seems to be failure personally.

Seek intimacy with God as the purpose of life.

Be a good intimate steward of resources. Cultivate results (be responsible).

Have a high sense of gratitude for what God does do.

Have a low sense of entitlement for results.

Appropriately rest (invest in relationships with God, self, and others).

Beth and I were working in our garden. It is actually a flower garden that we planted the year before. We had needed to do some work there for quite a while. Beth is the designer, and I am the implementer. She had flowers she wanted to plant, and I had weeds that needed to be pulled and mulch that needed to be replaced. It was difficult for us to individually set aside the time to do the work. We decided to work together on it even though we had different objectives to accomplish. For several hours we planted flowers, pulled weeds, scattered mulch, and hauled away dead branches and shrubs. Afterwards, we were tired and sore but encouraged about what we had accomplished. Beauty was once again restored to our flower garden!

But there was something more beautiful and lasting than the improvement of our flower garden. It was the joy and pleasure that Beth and I experienced with each other as we worked together.

She had a tool that she could push in the ground and, when pulled out, there was a hole just large enough for marigolds to be planted. There were hand-held tools for digging holes and other implements for removing the dirt. I was reminded of how Beth is a tool person – always having a device that is particularly suited to the task (whether that be sewing, writing, home improvements, or gardening). I love her for that uniqueness about her.

She was wearing a large floppy straw hat to protect her from the sun. On her hands were special gardening gloves. She was attired in a pair of old jeans and a faded buttoned-down shirt. A plastic bottle of water was at her side.

She worked on the large pots that held herbs and the portion of the garden where other herbs were planted. Peppermint, sage, oregano, lavender, parsley, basil, cilantro, and rosemary are scents with which she is familiar. She expertly uses those plants in preparing delicious-tasting food. I know very little about herbs, seem to keep forgetting their names, and have no idea what to do with them. I just know it smells nice when I walk by that portion of the garden.

Beth is special to me. Miss America in a swimsuit could not hold the allure to me that Beth does in her floppy hat, old jeans, gloves, and faded shirt. Her flair for design, smell, beauty, and order are exceptional and endear her to me.

I just enjoy being with Beth. She is such a joy and delight to be with. The amazing thing is that she told me how much she enjoyed being with me! That I could be a joy and delight to her was astounding to me.

The mutual joy and pleasure that we experienced with each other in our garden was of far greater value to us than the work that we accomplished. In fact, had there been no work to be done, there would have been an even a greater joy and pleasure in just relating well to each other. We have spent a lifetime cultivating our relationship with each other as a priority of our lives.

Life can be difficult, confusing, and wearisome, but I am Beth's and she is mine!

And so it is in our relationship with God. The greatest joy and pleasure there is in life is relating well to Him. It is the relational glory of oneness of experiencing Him and Him experiencing us – Christ in us, the hope of His glory. The boundary of Intimacy with God as the Purpose of Life must be firmly established and the relationship constantly cultivated in order for us to live life to its fullest.

For our destiny to be significant and enduring, we must have a relentless vision for the Boundary of Intimacy as Mission with God. As we labor diligently as good stewards who cultivate results, the Boundary of Intimate Stewardship of Resources helps us to understand that results are grace gifts from God. His grace in our lives and in our labors can be abundant or sufficient. Whatever the outcome, God is to be blessed, honored, respected, and valued. There is always something more important than results, and it is intimacy with God.

The Crucial Boundary of Rest helps us to always value person over performance, relationship as superior to accomplishment, character above competence, and who we are as more important than what we do. Without rest, our life becomes characterized by works, performance, obligation, and entitlement. We feel that there is so much that needs to be accomplished, and rest is a luxury that is reserved for the future. The war for the boundary of rest is experienced in daily battles to prioritize it over accomplishments. We must be intentional in pursuing the priority of rest. Otherwise, we will find ourselves as victims to our schedules, busyness, and time-consuming activities. The encouragement and enjoyment found in bonded relationships can slip through the fingers of our life when we are not intentional in pursuing them. When the Crucial Boundary of Rest is not kept, there is an emptiness we experience that no amount of accomplishment will remove. The relational glory of oneness with God, which is the purpose of life, is not experienced because we didn't have the time to do so.

God is saddened by our lack of priority of intimacy with Him. As we become older, our life is also characterized by sadness because of the intimacy that could have been with God and others. The reality is that intimacy has always been a much greater value and higher priority than accomplishment.

When we keep the Crucial Boundary of Rest, we are able to experience oneness of intimacy with God, intimacy as mission with Him, and results that are grace gifts from God.

When we keep the boundaries that cultivate our bonding with God, then we have purpose and destiny with Him. This is the purpose of our creation. There is no higher priority or calling in life than cultivating and experiencing intimacy with God. It is the eternal bond that God desires for us to experience with Him.

All of life is about coming to and acting upon the truth. I am His, and He is mine!

Discussion Questions

1. Which boundary that cultivates the eternal bond has been the most meaningful to you? Please explain.

2. What are practical things you can do to assure that intimacy with God is always a priority over mission with Him?

3. What roles do covenant relations with peers of the same gender play in cultivating relationship with God and protecting the boundaries that keep intimacy with Him?

4. What are the next best steps for you in experiencing the greatest joy and pleasure in life through cultivating intimacy with God as the purpose of life?

BIBLIOGRAPHY

Miriam Webster Collegiate Dictionary, 11th Edition

It Is Well with My Soul, Indonesianchurch.com

English, David A., *Banners of Bonding,* mail to david.english@cru.org

Kubler-Ross, Elisabeth, *On Death and Dying,* published 1969, Scribner, A division of Simon and Schuster, 1230 Avenue of the Americas, New York, New York, 10020

English, David A., *Phases of Life Studies,* for info contact Gravitation, larry@gravitationcreative.com

Cook, J. Roy, *One Hundred and One Famous Poems* (Chicago, IL; Contemporary Books, Inc. 1958)

Bright, William R., *First Love,* New life Publications, 2002, Peachtree, GA 30629

Saint Augustine, *The Confessions,* Loeb Classical Library, Harvard University Press

Pascal, Blaise, *Pensées* (New York; Penguin Books; 1995)

ChristianHistory.net, Hudson Taylor, faith missionary to China, posted 8/08/2008, 12:56pm

Meredith, Don, *Two Becoming One,* Moody Publishers, Chicago, Illinois, September 13, 1999

McGee, Robert, *Search for Significance,* Thomas Nelson Publisher, Nashville, Tennessee, May 5, 1998

Appendices

Appendix 1

Contrasting the World and the Kingdom of Heaven

The Kingdom of Heaven	The World
Grace	Works
Truth	Deception
Light	Darkness
Relationship	Accomplishment
Life	Death
Bonding	Isolation
Weakness	Strength
Failure	Success
Sacrifice	Lord Over
Vulnerable	Unapproachable
Serving Others	Being Served
Humility	Arrogance
Rest	Tired
Foolish	Puffed Up
Everything as loss	Everything as personal gain
Christ	World

Appendix 2

Steps to Developing a Covenant Team of Peers

1. Pray

2. Make a list of potential people

3. Prioritize the list of potential people according to the criteria for a covenant team.

Christ as their life / Confidentiality / Authenticity / Availability / Mutual Respect for each other / God and others focused

4. Talk to each person in order of priority (3-5 in number)

5. Set a time to get away for at least an overnight (Rendezvous*).

If you already have a team:

1. Appoint a facilitator.

2. Schedule opportunities to be together.

These could include weekly or monthly times to be with or communicate with each other. Between the times you rendezvous, you could keep in contact through monthly conference calls, email, monthly breakfasts, etc. However, these are not a substitute for a Rendezvous two to three times a year for at least an overnight.

3. In times of communication together, focus upon your relationship with God and the communication of your soul.

The purpose of the time together is not content. It is relationship. The easiest thing to do is to use the processing time you have scheduled to focus upon something that keeps them and you sharing what is really happening in your lives.

Pray for each other during your communication together. Pray for each other at least weekly.

Work at developing relational accountability.

4. Be sure the next Rendezvous is in your schedule.

    * Rendezvous is a time when a covenant team gets away for at least an overnight to share their life experiences authentically with each other in the context of intimacy with Christ as the purpose of life.

Appendix 3

Covenant Team of Peers and Kingdom Citizen Relationships

What They Are	What They Are Not
Relational Network	Program
Rendezvous	Meeting / Getaway
Mind-to-Mind Communication	Bible Study
Soul-to-Soul Communication	Book Study
Heart-to-Heart Communication	Share Group / E Team
Relational Accountability	Accountability Group
Life Shared with Covenant Brothers	Judgmental or Condemning
Real Relationship with God and Friends	Legalism or Heavy Doctrine
Reconciling the Public / Private Man	Double-minded or Deceptive
Iron Sharpening Iron	Rod of Correction
Filling a Male Relationship Void	Minimizing Family or Faith

Appendix 4

Perspectives of Intimate Stewardship of Resources

- Seek intimacy with God as the purpose of life.

- Focus upon unity of mission with God.

- Be a good intimate steward of resources (responsible).

- Dream and plan big.

- Appropriately rest (invest in relationships with God, self, and others).

- Have a low sense of entitlement (for what you thought or expected to happen).

- Have a high sense of gratitude (for what God did do).

- I am responsible for the depth, and God is responsible for the breadth (scope).

- Results are grace gifts from God.

- Don't take what seems to be failure personally.

Appendix 5

Principles of Intimate Stewardship of Resources

1. Our spiritual relationship with God should be more important than the physical provisions (resources) He gives us.

2. God is far more concerned about our intimacy with Him than He is with the resources He gives to us.

3. Character is a higher priority than stewardship. We are to be above reproach in who we are and in what we do. (Titus 1:5-9)

4. Our dreams will exceed the resources God provides. Grace gifts from God are the way God fulfills dreams we have that exceed the resources that have been provided.

5. If we labor apart from God and outside the resources that God provides (irresponsibility), then we are poor stewards; and we lose our testimony and potentially our opportunity to labor in the Kingdom of God.

6. Our view of God determines how we will use resources. (Matthew 25:14-30)

7. All the resources are God's. He is the ultimate resource generator. (Psalm 50:10)

8. God can do a lot with little resources. (Matthew 14:13-21, Judges 7:2-25)

Appendix 6

Joy Is the Authenticator
of the Eternal Bond

1. The oneness of intimate relationship with God is the priority of life. It results in the greatest joy and pleasure we can experience. (Psalm 16:11, 1 Peter 1:8)

2. Oneness of intimacy of relationship is a greater priority and greater joy than intimacy as mission. (Revelation 2:2-4)

3. God is more delighted in intimacy as mission with Him than He is with the results accomplished. (Luke 10:38-42)

4. The shared joy of intimacy of relationship and intimacy as mission with God are greater joys than the joy of intimate stewardship of resources. (Luke 10:38-42)

5. There is a shared joy (between God and us) in intimate stewardship of resources. (Matthew 25:21, 23)

6. The authenticator of intimacy as mission is not phenomenon. It is joy in and with the Lord. (Luke 10:17-20)

7. The true authenticator of intimate stewardship of resources is joy and pleasure in oneness with God rather than in ministry phenomenon. (Luke 10:38-42)

Appendix 7

Rest Is an Essential of Intimacy

1. Rest invests in person, not performance.

2. Rest helps us to focus upon who we are as more important than what we do.

3. Rest helps the joy of intimacy to always be the priority over joy of accomplishment.

4. Rest is the authenticator of whether we understand the priority of relationships (covenant relationships) over mission and resources (stewardship).

Appendix 8

Relational Values that God Constantly Communicates to Us

1. I love you whether you are winning or losing.

2. I desire relationship with you, not perfection from you.

3. I am not trying to fix you.

4. The character of your person is more important to Me than the competency of what you do.

5. Who you are in intimacy with Me is of far greater value to Me than any position to which you might attain, any scope of responsibility that you could be given, or any task that you might ever perform.

6. Who you are is more important to Me than what you do.

7. My greatest joy and pleasure is to experience who you are as we walk together through the great adventure of life that we share with each other in an eternal bond.

Connect with Us

Please visit us online. We appreciate you and would love to connect and stay in touch with you. David and his team have developed a website to provide information, updates, resources, and how to order additional books and materials. It is designed to encourage and challenge you to live fully.

www.DavidAEnglish.com

Books and Materials

The Eternal Bond

This book makes an excellent gift. It is also ideal for use it in a small group setting (it was beta tested in small groups). There is even a leaders guide that walks you through using *The Eternal Bond* in a small group.

Phases of a Man's Life Books

David English has written a series of books that help men process the struggles of life and make better decisions. Although the books were originally aimed at men, the principles apply for women as well. They are great for individual self study and/or small groups of peers.

The Defining Decisions (ages 17 to 22)

Brilliant insight into important life choices that shape character and a life that transcends self.

Entering The Adult World (ages 23 to 28)

We want to explore life and not be pinned down to long-term decisions. At the same time, we want to establish some roots and stability.

Minor Life Transition (ages 29 to 32)

We want the uncertainty of the future to be cleared up and our direction in life to bring satisfaction now.

Priority Decision Phase (ages 33 to 39)

We are faced as never before with having to decide which aspects of our life are most important and if we will commit the time it takes to truly reflect them.

Major Life Transition (ages 40 to 45)

This phase is best described as the "Wounded Warrior." The wounds are emotional, but a man's future is determined by how he deals with his wounds.

Mature Adult (ages 46 to 54)

This is a period of time in our lives in which we are being shaped and formed in a way that will ultimately lead to our greatest years of effectiveness.

Legacy Phase (ages 55 to 70)

It is during this phase of our live that we will have our greatest years of effectiveness. We greatly desire to live a life of significance.

Sage Phase (ages 71 up)

As we reach our 70s our ability to influence and be effective in the lives of others is now totally dependent upon our person.

Phases of Life Chart

This full color 17 x 22 inch poster is a companion piece to all of the Phases of a Man's Life books. This chart quickly gives a working overview of each phase of life and identifies Emotional/Developmental Tasks with recommended Necessary Next Steps.

God desires to cultivate His relationship with you.
David English's books and materials are great personal tools to help you focus your eternal bond with God.

Order David's Books and Materials Online

www.DavidAEnglish.com

Things don't always work, so we have a back-up. If you need to order books and materials and are having trouble with the website, email our materials guy, Larry Thompson, at Larry@gravitationcreative.com or call him at 919-810-9088. He really will assist you and help you get what you need.